Cook's Corner

Everyday
Chinese

igloobooks

Published in 2018
by Igloo Books Ltd
Cottage Farm
Sywell
NN6 0BJ
www.igloobooks.com

All imagery: © iStock / Getty Images

STA002 0218
2 4 6 8 10 9 7 5 3 1
ISBN: 978-1-78810-185-1

Cover designed by Nicholas Gage
Interiors designed by Simon Parker
Edited by Jasmin Peppiatt

Printed and manufactured in China

Cook's Corner

Everyday
Chinese

Contents

Cook's Corner

Everyday Chinese
Meat dishes

Spicy egg and prawn noodles

SERVES: 2 | PREP TIME: 30 MINUTES | COOKING TIME: 20 MINUTES

INGREDIENTS

150 g / 5 ¼ oz rice vermicelli

2 eggs, beaten

1 tsp curry powder

2 tbsp sesame oil

180 g / 6 ¼ oz raw king prawns, shelled

1 in piece of root ginger, grated

1 birds eye chilli (chili), chopped

1 red pepper, thinly sliced

1 green pepper, thinly sliced

¼ white cabbage, shredded

200 ml / 7 fl. oz / ¾ cup chicken stock

1 tbsp sesame seeds

METHOD

1. Cook the noodles in a pan of boiling water for 1-2 minutes until softened. Drain and rinse with cold water and set aside.

2. Whisk the eggs with a pinch of curry powder. Heat half the oil in a wok and cook the egg for 2-3 minutes until they resemble an omelette. Remove from the pan and roughly chop.

3. Add the remaining oil to the pan and cook the prawns for 1 minute before adding the remaining curry powder, ginger, chilli, peppers and cabbage. Continue cooking for 2-3 minutes until fragrant, stirring continuously.

4. Add the noodles back into the pan and add the chicken stock. Continue to stir-fry until most of the liquid has been absorbed and the noodles are tender. Mix through the egg to warm through.

5. Divide between two serving plates and scatter over the sesame seeds.

Shanghai soup dumplings

MAKES: 40 | PREP TIME: 4 HOURS | COOKING TIME: 8 MINUTES

INGREDIENTS

1 chicken carcass, broken into pieces

1 small ham hock

2 tbsp fresh root ginger, sliced

1 tbsp white peppercorns

6 spring onions (scallions), finely chopped

300 g / 10 ½ oz / 2 cups plain (all-purpose) flour

150 g / 5 ½ oz / 1 cup minced pork

150 g / 5 ½ oz / 1 cup raw prawns (shrimp), finely chopped

1 tbsp Shaoxing rice wine

1 tbsp light soy sauce

2 tsp caster (superfine) sugar

coriander (cilantro) leaves, to garnish

METHOD

1. Put the chicken carcass and ham hock in a large saucepan with the ginger, peppercorns and two thirds of the spring onions. Add enough cold water to just cover the ingredients, then bring to the boil. Reduce the heat and simmer for 3 hours, then strain into a plastic container. Leave to cool, then refrigerate overnight.

2. Sift the flour into a bowl and stir in 250 ml of recently boiled water. Knead for 8 minutes or until smooth, adding more flour if necessary. Rest for 30 minutes.

3. Meanwhile, put the pork, prawns, rice wine, soy sauce, sugar, and the rest of the spring onions in a food processor and pulse to a paste. Add 250 ml of the jellied stock and blend again, then chill until ready to use.

4. Divide the rested dough into 40 balls, then flatten them. Add 1 tablespoon of filling to each wrapper, pleating round the outside and pinching to seal in the centre.

5. Space out the dumplings in oiled steamer baskets and steam for 8 minutes. Serve immediately, garnished with coriander, being careful not to pierce them.

Chicken and snake beans

SERVES: 2 | PREP TIME: 5 MINUTES | COOKING TIME: 12 MINUTES

INGREDIENTS

2 tbsp vegetable oil

1 red onion, sliced

2 cloves of garlic, thinly sliced

1 tbsp root ginger, thinly sliced

2 skinless chicken breasts, sliced

6 young snake beans, halved if very long

2 tbsp light soy sauce

1 small carrot, spiralized or julienned

50 g / 1 ¾ oz / 1 cup bean sprouts

METHOD

1. Heat the oil in a large wok and fry the onion, garlic and ginger for 2 minutes.

2. Add the chicken and stir-fry for 3 minutes or until lightly coloured. Add the snake beans and stir-fry for 1 minute.

3. Add the soy sauce and 40 ml of water, then cover and steam for 4 minutes.

4. Add the carrot and bean sprouts and stir-fry for 2 minutes, then serve immediately.

Beef, egg and choi sum with rice

SERVES: 4 | PREP TIME: 15 MINUTES | COOKING TIME: 10-14 MINUTES

INGREDIENTS

2 tbsp vegetable oil

1 clove of garlic, crushed

1 tsp fresh root ginger, finely grated

1 small sirloin steak, very thinly sliced

1 tbsp Shaoxing rice wine

1 tbsp oyster sauce

30 g / 1 oz / 1 cup choi sum, cut into short lengths

2 medium eggs

½ tsp light soy sauce

steamed rice, to serve

METHOD

1. Heat 1 tablespoon of the oil in a wok and fry the garlic and ginger for 1 minute. Add the steak and stir-fry for 2 minutes. Add the rice wine and oyster sauce and stir-fry for 1 minute. Cover and set aside.

2. Meanwhile, steam the choi sum for 2 minutes or until just tender.

3. Heat the rest of the oil in a frying pan. Beat the eggs with the soy sauce, then pour it into the pan and swirl to coat the bottom. Cook until just set, then turn the omelette out onto a chopping board and slice it into ribbons.

4. Serve the beef, omelette and choi sum on a bed of steamed rice.

Pork and prawn siu mai

MAKES:: 24 | PREP TIME: 4 MINUTES | COOKING TIME: 12 MINUTES

INGREDIENTS

350 g / 12 ½ oz / 2 ⅓ cups minced pork

175 g / 6 oz / 1 ¼ cups raw prawns (shrimp), finely chopped

50 g / 1 ¾ oz / ½ cup canned water chestnuts, finely chopped

2 spring onions (scallions), finely chopped

1 tsp fresh root ginger, finely grated

1 ½ tbsp Shaoxing rice wine

2 tbsp light soy sauce

2 tsp sesame oil

1 ½ tbsp cornflour (cornstarch)

24 round egg wonton wrappers

1 egg white, beaten

24 salmon eggs

METHOD

1. Mix the pork with the prawns, water chestnuts, spring onions, ginger, rice wine, soy sauce, sesame oil and cornflour. Season with 1 teaspoon of salt and some freshly ground white pepper.

2. Put 1 tablespoon of filling in the centre of each wonton wrapper, then brush round the edge with egg white. Gather up the edges and squeeze gently to seal, then top each one with a single salmon egg.

3. Space out the siu mai in oiled steamer baskets and steam for 12 minutes, then serve immediately.

Satay beef noodle soup

SERVES: 4 | PREP TIME: 10 MINUTES | COOKING TIME: 15 MINUTES

INGREDIENTS

75 g / 2 ½ oz / ⅓ cup smooth peanut butter

1 tbsp runny honey

2 tbsp dark soy sauce

1 tsp Chinese five spice

1 clove of garlic, crushed

300 g / 10 ½ oz rump steak, thinly sliced

300 g / 10 ½ oz thin rice noodles

2 tbsp vegetable oil

2 red chillies (chilies), chopped

2 tsp fresh root ginger, finely chopped

½ green pepper, diced

150 g / 5 ½ oz / 1 cup canned pineapple, diced

1 litre / 1 pint 14 fl. oz / 4 cups beef stock

METHOD

1. Mix the peanut butter with the honey, soy sauce, five spice and garlic. Add the steak and stir well to coat, then marinate in the fridge for 3 hours.

2. Cook the noodles in boiling water according to the packet instructions or until al dente. Drain well and divide between four bowls.

3. Heat the oil in a wok and stir-fry the chillies and ginger for 1 minute. Add the green pepper and stir-fry for 2 minutes.

4. Add the beef and marinade and stir-fry for 3 minutes or until just cooked. Add the pineapple and stock and bring to a simmer, then ladle over the noodles and serve immediately.

15

Sweet and sour chicken

SERVES: 2 | PREP TIME: 2 MINUTES | COOKING TIME: 10 MINUTES

INGREDIENTS

80 g / 2 ¾ oz / ⅓ cup short-grain rice

1 tbsp rice wine vinegar

2 tbsp tomato purée

1 tsp soy sauce

200 g / 7 oz / 1 ¼ cups pineapple chunks in juice

1 tsp soft brown sugar

1 tbsp vegetable oil

250 g / 9 oz chicken breast, sliced

1 red chilli (chili), deseeded and sliced

2 tsp cornflour (cornstarch)

METHOD

1. Cook the rice as per the packet instructions and set aside until required.

2. Combine the vinegar, tomato purée, soy, pineapple juice and sugar and whisk to combine.

3. Heat the oil in a wok or frying pan over a medium high heat. Add the chicken and brown, cooking for 4-5 minutes. Add the chilli and pineapple chunks to the pan and continue to stir-fry for a further 2-3 minutes.

4. Add the liquid to the pan and leave to bubble and reduce for 1-2 minutes. Mix the cornflour with a little water to form a paste. Mix through the chicken to thicken.

5. Serve with the rice.

Stir-fry pork noodles

SERVES: 2 | PREP TIME: 15 MINUTES | COOKING TIME: 15 MINUTES

INGREDIENTS

2 tbsp soy sauce

1 tsp Chinese five spice

1 tsp toasted sesame oil

1 lime, juice and zest

1 tsp honey

300 g / 10 ½ oz diced pork

150 g / 5 ¼ oz flat egg noodles

3 spring onions (scallions), sliced

2 tsp black sesame seeds

METHOD

1. Combine the soy, five spice, sesame oil, lime and honey in a large bowl. Add the pork to the marinade and mix to coat the meat. Cover and leave to marinade for 10 minutes.

2. Heat a non-stick frying pan over a medium high heat. Once hot add the pork and stir-fry for 12-15 minutes until firm and cooked through. At the same time, cook the noodles as per the packet instructions.

3. Add the noodles to the pork and mix through to coat the noodles in the sauce.

4. Mix through the spring onions before adding to serving plates and scattering over the sesame seeds.

17

Crispy chilli beef

SERVES: 4 | PREP TIME: 15 MINUTES | COOKING TIME: 10 MINUTES

INGREDIENTS

175 ml / 6 fl. oz / ⅔ cup pineapple juice

100 ml / 3 ½ fl. oz / ½ cup sweet
chilli sauce

1 tbsp light soy sauce

450 g / 1 lb minute steak,
very thinly sliced

1 tsp Chinese five spice

100 g / 3 ½ oz / ⅔ cup cornflour (cornstarch)

vegetable oil, for deep-frying

2 spring onions (scallions), sliced

METHOD

1. To make the sauce, put the pineapple juice,
   chilli sauce and soy sauce in a small pan.
   Bring to the boil and cook until reduced.

2. Season the beef with salt and five spice, then
   toss it with the cornflour, squeezing to
   ensure it adheres well.

3. Heat the oil in a deep fat fryer, according to
   the manufacturer's instructions, to a
   temperature of 180°C (350F).

4. Deep fry the beef in two batches for
   4 minutes or until very crisp. Drain the
   beef on plenty of kitchen paper, then toss
   it with the sauce.

5. Sprinkle the beef with spring onions and
   serve immediately.

Fried chicken wing drumettes

SERVES: 4 | PREP TIME: 15 MINUTES | COOKING TIME: 6 MINUTES

INGREDIENTS

vegetable oil, for deep frying

75 g / 2 ½ oz / ½ cup plain (all-purpose) flour

½ tsp Chinese five spice

1 large egg, separated

150 ml / 5 ½ fl. oz / ⅔ cup sparkling water

2 tbsp black sesame seeds

12 large chicken wing drumettes

METHOD

1. Heat the oil in a deep fat fryer, according to the manufacturer's instructions, to a temperature of 180°C (350F).

2. Mix 60 g of flour with the five spice and a pinch of salt and make a well in the middle. Add the egg yolk and sparkling water, then whisk them together, gradually incorporating all the flour from round the outside. Whip the egg white until stiff, then fold it into the batter with the sesame seeds.

3. Toss the chicken with the rest of the flour and shake off any excess. Working in batches, dip the chicken in the batter, then deep-fry for 6 minutes or until brown and cooked through. Drain on kitchen paper and serve immediately.

19

Asian beef tacos

SERVES: 2 | PREP TIME: 15 MINUTES | COOKING TIME: 15 MINUTES

INGREDIENTS

200 g / 7 oz beef frying steak, sliced

1 tsp Chinese five spice

1 clove of garlic, minced

1 tsp red chilli (chili) paste

1 tbsp hoisin sauce

1 tsp soy sauce

1 tbsp sesame oil

4 spring onions (scallions), sliced

2 corn tortillas

1 red onion, sliced

½ cucumber, sliced

50 g / 1 ¾ oz salad leaves

METHOD

1. Combine the beef with the five spice, garlic, chilli paste, hoisin and soy. Mix well to combine and coat the meat before leaving for 10 minutes.

2. Heat the oil in a frying pan or wok over a medium high heat. Once the oil is smoking, add the beef and stir-fry for 12-15 minutes. Add the spring onions to the pan after 10 minutes.

3. Place the tortillas onto a clean dry surface and fill with the beef, red onion, cucumber and salad.

4. Serve with a hot sauce for an extra spicy hit.

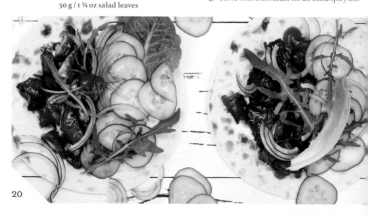

Turkey noodle soup

SERVES: 4 | PREP TIME: 10 MINUTES | COOKING TIME: 15 MINUTES

INGREDIENTS

4 large eggs

300 g / 10 ½ oz thin egg noodles

1 litre / 1 pint 14 fl. oz / 4 cups chicken stock

2 tbsp Shaoxing rice wine

1 tsp caster (superfine) sugar

2 tbsp dark soy sauce

2 turkey breast fillets

3 spring onions (scallions), chopped,
green parts only

2 tsp chilli (chili) flakes

METHOD

1. Put the eggs in a saucepan of cold water and bring to the boil. Reduce the heat and simmer gently for 5 minutes, then plunge into iced water. Wait for 5 minutes, then peel and halve the eggs.

2. Meanwhile, cook the noodles according to instructions. Divide between four bowls.

3. Heat the stock in a saucepan with the rice wine, sugar and soy sauce. When it starts to boil, add the turkey and poach gently for 6 minutes. Remove the turkey from the broth and cut it into slices, then arrange on top of the noodles.

4. Season the broth to taste, then ladle it over the noodles and garnish with the eggs, spring onion greens and chilli flakes.

Crispy duck rolls

MAKES: 16 | PREP TIME: 20 MINUTES | COOKING TIME: 4 MINUTES

INGREDIENTS

½ Cantonese roast duck, boned, shredded and cooled

2 tbsp hoisin sauce

4 spring onions (scallions), finely julienned

200 g / 7 oz / 1 cup canned bamboo shoots, drained and finely julienned

16 small spring roll wrappers

1 tsp cornflour, mixed with 1 tbsp boiling water

vegetable oil, for deep frying

METHOD

1. Mix the duck with the hoisin, spring onions and bamboo shoots.

2. Divide the mixture between the spring roll wrappers. Fold up the bottom corner, then fold in the sides. Brush the top corner with some of the cornflour glue, then roll them up tightly into a cigar shape.

3. Heat the vegetable oil in a deep fat fryer to a temperature of 180°C (350F).

4. Fry the rolls in batches for 4 minutes or until golden and crisp. Drain on plenty of kitchen paper and serve immediately.

Sticky chicken wings

SERVES: 2-4 | PREP TIME: 20 MINUTES | COOKING TIME: 45 MINUTES

INGREDIENTS

1 kg / 2lbs 3 oz chicken wings

1 tbsp Chinese five spice

2 cloves of garlic, minced

1 red chilli (chili), chopped

2 tbsp sesame oil

1 tsp honey

1 tbsp dark soy sauce

1 tsp rice vinegar

METHOD

1. Preheat the oven to 180°C (160°C fan) / 350F / gas 4 and line a baking tray with foil.

2. Place the chicken wings in a large mixing bowl. Whisk together the remaining ingredients until well combined. Pour over the chicken wings and toss to coat and set aside for 20 minutes.

3. Shake off any excess marinade and place the chicken on to the prepared baking tray, reserving the excess marinade for basting.

4. Place into the oven and cook for 40-45 minutes, basting a couple times with the reserved marinade. The wings will be ready when the meat is falling from the bones and the wings are starting to char at the edges.

23

Stir-fried beef with crunchy vegetables

SERVES: 4 | PREP TIME: 5 MINUTES | COOKING TIME: 15 MINUTES

INGREDIENTS

2 tbsp vegetable oil

1 clove of garlic, squashed

1 sirloin steak, thinly sliced

2 tbsp dark soy sauce

1 small red onion, cut into wedges

1 small carrot, peeled and sliced diagonally

1 small red pepper, deseeded and sliced

1 small yellow pepper, deseeded and sliced

½ head broccoli, cut into florets

100 g / 3 ½ oz / ⅔ cup green beans, trimmed and halved

100 g / 3 ½ oz / ⅔ cup mangetout

1 pak choi, sliced

75 ml / 2 ½ fl. oz / ⅓ cup Shaoxing rice wine

METHOD

1. Heat the oil in a large wok and stir-fry the garlic for 2 minutes. Remove with a slotted spoon and discard.

2. Add the steak and stir-fry for 4 minutes or until it starts to colour. Pour in the soy sauce and stir-fry until it has coated the beef and almost evaporated.

3. Add the onion and carrot and stir-fry over a high heat for 1 minute. Add the peppers and broccoli and stir-fry for 1 minute. Add the green beans, mangetout and pak choi and stir-fry for 1 minute.

4. Pour in the rice wine and stir-fry for 2 minutes, then serve immediately.

Char siu pork noodle soup

SERVES: 6 | PREP TIME: 20 MINUTES + OVERNIGHT | COOKING TIME: 25 MINUTE

INGREDIENTS

2 tbsp hoisin sauce

2 tbsp sweet soy sauce or kecap manis

2 tbsp runny honey

1 tsp Chinese five spice

1 tbsp vegetable oil

1 tsp sesame oil

a few drops red food colouring

450 g / 1 lb whole pork tenderloin

1.2 litres / 2 pints / 4 ¾ cups pork or chicken stock

400 g / 14 oz thin egg noodles

4 slices leftover roast pork belly,
cut into bite-sized pieces

4 spring onions (scallions), sliced, green parts only

1 small bunch fresh coriander
(cilantro), chopped

METHOD

1. Put the hoisin, soy, honey, five spice, vegetable oil, sesame oil and food colouring in a saucepan. Stir continuously while it comes to the boil, then leave to cool. Scrape the mixture into a freezer bag, add the pork and massage well to coat. Marinate in the fridge overnight.

2. Preheat the oven to 180°C (160°C fan) / 350F / gas 4 and line a roasting tin with greaseproof paper. Transfer the pork to the tin and roast for 25 minutes, basting with marinade twice, part way through.

3. Meanwhile, heat the stock in a saucepan. Cook the noodles in boiling water according to packet instructions, then drain and divide between six warm bowls. Slice the pork tenderloin and divide between the bowls and add some pork belly and spring onion greens to each one.

4. Ladle over the stock, sprinkle with coriander and serve immediately.

Chicken curry

SERVES: 4 | PREP TIME: 5 MINUTES | COOKING TIME: 18 MINUTES

INGREDIENTS

50 g / 1 ¾ oz / ¼ cup butter

30 g / 1 oz / ¼ cup plain (all-purpose) flour

2 tsp Madras curry powder

2 tsp Chinese five spice

1 tsp ground ginger

1 tsp garlic powder

500 ml / 17 ½ fl. oz / 2 cups chicken stock

2 tbsp vegetable oil

2 cloves of garlic, crushed

1 tbsp fresh root ginger, finely chopped

kinless chicken breasts, cut into bite-sized pieces

1 onion, diced

1 red pepper, deseeded and sliced

steamed rice, to serve

flat-leaf parsley, to garnish

METHOD

1. To make the curry sauce, melt the butter in a saucepan, then stir in the flour, curry powder, five spice, ground ginger and garlic powder. Stir over a gentle heat for 2 minutes, then gradually incorporate the stock. Continue stirring until the mixture simmers and thickens, then take the pan off the heat.

2. Heat the vegetable oil in a large wok and stir-fry the garlic and ginger for 1 minute. Add the chicken and stir-fry for 3 minutes or until opaque on the outside.

3. Add the onion and peppers and stir-fry for 2 minutes, then pour in the curry sauce.

4. Simmer for 4 minutes, stirring regularly, or until the chicken is cooked through.

5. Serve the curry on a bed of steamed rice, garnished with parsley.

Cantonese roast duck

SERVES: 6 | PREP TIME: 30 MINUTES | COOKING TIME: 1 HOUR, 20 MINUTES

INGREDIENTS

1.8 kg / 4 lb whole duck

1 tbsp vegetable oil

75 ml / 2 ½ fl. oz / ⅓ cup dark soy sauce

100 ml / 3 ½ fl. oz / ½ cup Shaoxing
rice wine

1 tbsp demerara sugar

2 tbsp rice wine vinegar

4 cloves of garlic, squashed

4 slices fresh root ginger

4 spring onions (scallions), chopped

2 star anise

4 pieces dried orange peel

6 cloves

1 tbsp white peppercorns

2 tbsp runny honey

METHOD

1. Rub the duck inside and out with
1 tbsp of salt. Heat the oil in a large wok and
swirl to coat, then sear the duck all over until
nicely browned.

2. Put the soy sauce, rice wine, sugar, vinegar,
garlic, ginger, spring onion whites, star
anise, cloves and peppercorns in a saucepan
large enough to accommodate the duck. Stir
in 750 ml of water.

3. Bring to the boil, then carefully lower
in the duck, breast side down. Cover and
simmer gently for 1 hour, turning the duck
every 15 minutes.

4. Preheat the oven to 220°C (200°C fan) / 425F /
gas 7. Transfer the duck to a trivet inside a
large roasting tin. Dry the skin well with
kitchen paper.

5. Roast the duck for 10 minutes.
Brush the duck all over with honey, then
return to the oven for 10 minutes or until the
skin is nicely lacquered.

6. Leave the duck to rest for 15 minutes, then
remove the meat from the bones and cut
into slices.

30

Meatball noodles with pineapple

SERVES: 4 | PREP TIME: 45 MINUTES | COOKING TIME: 20 MINUTES

INGREDIENTS

450 g / 1 lb / 3 cups minced pork

1 tsp fresh root ginger, finely grated

4 spring onions (scallions), whites finely chopped, greens sliced

50 ml / 1 ¾ fl. oz / ¼ cup Shaoxing rice wine

3 tbsp kecap manis

1 tbsp sesame oil

3 medium eggs, beaten

1 tbsp cornflour (cornstarch)

100 g / 3 ½ oz / 1 cup panko breadcrumbs

2 tbsp vegetable oil

30 g / 1 oz / ¼ cup cashew nuts

1 large red chilli (chili), sliced

400 g / 14 fl. oz / 2 cups canned pineapple chunks in juice

400 g / 14 oz flat wheat noodles

sesame seeds and coriander (cilantro) leaves, to serve

METHOD

1. Put the pork in a large mixing bowl and beat in 60 ml of cold water. Add the ginger and spring onion whites and mix well.

2. Whisk the rice wine with the kecap manis, sesame oil and eggs, then slowly incorporate it into the pork mixture. Mix the cornflour with the breadcrumbs, then work it into the pork.

3. Shape the mixture into 16 meatballs, then cover and chill in the fridge for 30 minutes.

4. Heat the vegetable oil in a frying pan and sear the meatballs until browned all over.

5. Add the cashew nuts and chilli and cook until the cashews are golden brown. Add the pineapple and its juice, then cover and simmer for 5 minutes.

6. Meanwhile, cook the noodles according to the packet instructions. Toss the noodles with the meatballs and sauce and serve garnished with sesame seeds and coriander leaves.

Sweet and sour chicken balls

SERVES: 4 | PREP TIME: 30 MINUTES | COOKING TIME: 4 MINUTES

INGREDIENTS

75 g / 2 ½ oz / ½ cup plain (all-purpose) flour

75 g / 2 ½ oz / ½ cup cornflour (cornstarch)

1 tsp baking powder

1 tsp caster (superfine) sugar

1 tsp sesame oil

vegetable oil, for deep-frying

4 skinless chicken breasts, cut into bite-sized chunks

FOR THE SAUCE:

125 ml / 4 ½ fl. oz / ½ cup pineapple juice

50 ml / 1 ¾ fl. oz / ¼ cup tomato ketchup

2 tbsp rice wine vinegar

2 tbsp light brown sugar

1 tsp soy sauce

1 tbsp cornflour (cornstarch)

METHOD

1. To make the sauce, heat the pineapple juice, ketchup, vinegar, sugar and soy sauce together in a small saucepan. Slake the cornflour with 3 tablespoons of cold water, then stir it into the saucepan. Continue to stir over a medium heat until the sauce simmers and thickens. Transfer to serving pots and leave to cool.

2. Sieve the flour, cornflour, baking powder and sugar together. Stir the sesame oil into 150 ml of cold water, then whisk it into the flour to form a batter.

3. Heat the vegetable oil in a deep fat fryer, according to the manufacturer's instructions, to a temperature of 180°C (350F).

4. Dip the chicken breast chunks in batter and deep fry for 4 minutes or until nicely browned.

5. Drain the chicken on plenty of kitchen paper and serve with the sweet and sour sauce for dipping.

Lemon beef stir-fry

SERVES: 4 | PREP TIME: 5 MINUTES | COOKING TIME: 10 MINUTES

INGREDIENTS

2 tbsp vegetable oil

1 tbsp fresh root ginger, finely grated

1 sirloin steak, thinly sliced

2 sticks celery, sliced

4 spring onions, sliced

1 green pepper, cubed

1 red pepper, cubed

1 head broccoli, cut into florets

1 ½ lemons, juiced

2 tsp cornflour (cornstarch)

1 tbsp caster (superfine) sugar

2 tbsp light soy sauce

METHOD

1. Heat the oil in a large wok and stir-fry the ginger for 1 minute.

2. Add the steak and stir-fry for 3 minutes.

3. Add the vegetables and stir-fry over a high heat for 4 minutes.

4. Mix the lemon juice with the cornflour, sugar, soy sauce and 50 ml of water, then pour it into the wok and stir-fry for 2 minutes. Serve immediately.

Chicken and vegetable fried rice

SERVES: 4 | PREP TIME: 5 MINUTES | COOKING TIME: 12 MINUTES

INGREDIENTS

2 tbsp vegetable oil
1 small onion, sliced
2 cloves of garlic, thinly sliced
1 tbsp root ginger, thinly sliced
orange pepper, deseeded, quartered and sliced
1 head broccoli, cut into florets
1 courgette (zucchini), thinly sliced
50 ml / 1 ¾ fl. oz / ¼ cup Shaoxing rice wine
old roast chicken breasts, skinned and chopped
75 g / 2 ½ oz / ½ cup frozen peas, defrosted
500 g / 17 ½ oz / 3 cups long-grain rice, cooked
2 tbsp light soy sauce
2 tsp sesame oil

METHOD

1. Heat the vegetable oil in a large wok and fry the onion, garlic and ginger for 1 minute.

2. Add the vegetables and fry for 4 minutes. Pour over the rice wine, then cover and steam for 2 minutes.

3. Add the chicken, peas and rice and stir-fry for 4 minutes or until piping hot. Season the rice with soy sauce and sesame oil, then divide between four plates and serve immediately.

Beef noodle soup

SERVES: 2 | PREP TIME: 10 MINUTES | COOKING TIME: 30 MINUTES

INGREDIENTS

750 ml / 25 fl. oz / 3 cups beef stock

1 in piece of root ginger, grated

2 cloves of garlic, sliced

1 tbsp sesame oil

1 tbsp soy sauce

2 limes, juiced

300 g / 10 ½ oz egg noodles

300 g / 10 ½ oz fillet steak, thinly sliced

handful of coriander (cilantro), chopped

2 tbsp chives, chopped

METHOD

1. Place the stock into a saucepan and add the ginger, garlic, sesame, soy and lime juice. Heat until boiling before turning down to a simmer and covering. Leave for 8-10 minutes.

2. Cook the noodles as per the packet instructions, then drain and divide between serving bowls.

3. To cook the beef, drop directly into the hot soup. It will need no more than a minute to cook as you want it to still be pink.

4. Spoon the beef soup over the noodles and garnish with the chopped herbs.

Quinoa and sausage spring rolls

MAKES: 6 | PREP TIME: 45 MINUTES | COOKING TIME: 5 MINUTES

INGREDIENTS

150 g / 5 ½ oz / ¾ cup quinoa

1 tbsp vegetable oil

1 clove of garlic, crushed

1 tsp fresh root ginger, finely grated

1 Chinese sausage, diced

1 small courgette (zucchini), diced

½ yellow pepper, finely chopped

6 rice paper wrappers

vegetable oil, for deep frying

coriander (cilantro), to garnish

METHOD

1. Put the quinoa in a saucepan with 150 ml water. Cover and simmer for 10 minutes, then leave to stand for a further 15 minutes.

2. Heat the vegetable oil in a wok and stir-fry the garlic and ginger for 30 seconds. Add the sausage, zucchini and pepper and stir-fry for 3 minutes. Take the pan off the heat and stir in the quinoa.

3. Dip the first rice paper wrapper in a bowl of cold water, then lay out on a clean chopping board. Spoon a sixth of the filling on top. Fold over the sides of the wrapper, then roll it up. Repeat to form six rolls.

4. Deep fry the spring rolls in two batches for 5 minutes at 180°C (350 F). Drain on kitchen paper, garnish with coriander and serve.

Chicken and vegetable soup

SERVES: 2-4 | PREP TIME: 15 MINUTES | COOKING TIME: 20 MINUTES

INGREDIENTS

500 ml / 17 fl. oz / 2 cups chicken stock

15 g / ½ oz ginger, sliced

2 cloves of garlic, sliced

1 star anise

½ cinnamon stick

1 tsp chilli (chili) flakes

1 tbsp soy sauce

200 g / 7 oz chicken breast, sliced

50 g / 1 ¾ oz spring greens

150 g / 5 ¼ oz mixed vegetables

4 spring onions (scallions), halved

METHOD

1. Place the stock into a saucepan with the ginger, garlic, star anise, cinnamon, chilli and soy. Heat until boiling before turning down to a simmer. Cover and cook for 10 minutes to let the flavours infuse.

2. Add the chicken to the pan and cook for a further 8-10 minutes until it has changed colour and firmed.

3. Add the vegetables and spring onions to the soup and continue to cook for 5-6 minutes until tender.

4. Spoon the soup into serving bowls.

Braised beef with noodles

SERVES: 4 | PREP TIME: 5 MINUTES | COOKING TIME: 2 HOURS, 15 MINUTES

INGREDIENTS

600 g / 1 lb 5 ½ oz braising steak, cut into
bite-sized chunks

1 tsp Chinese five spice

2 tbsp vegetable oil

1 tbsp runny honey

3 tbsp Shaoxing rice wine

1 tbsp light soy sauce

½ tbsp dark soy sauce

400 g / 14 oz medium egg noodles

coriander (cilantro), to garnish

METHOD

1. Dry the beef thoroughly with kitchen paper, then season with salt and the five spice.

2. Heat the vegetable oil in a wok, add the beef and stir-fry for 4 minutes. Drizzle with honey and stir-fry until browned. Add the rice wine, soy sauces and 500 ml of water.

3. Cover and simmer gently for 2 hours or until tender, stirring occasionally. Cook the noodles according to the packet instructions or until al dente, then drain well.

4. Stir the noodles into the beef pan, then divide between four warm bowls and serve immediately, garnished with coriander.

41

Chicken salad open wontons

SERVES: 4 | PREP TIME: 10 MINUTES | COOKING TIME: 10 MINUTES

INGREDIENTS

12 wonton wrappers

2 tbsp vegetable oil

1 clove of garlic, crushed

2 tsp fresh root ginger, finely grated

3 skinless boneless chicken thighs, diced

1 tbsp oyster sauce

1 tsp sesame oil

½ red onion, finely diced

2 medium tomatoes,
deseeded and finely diced

½ green pepper, deseeded and diced

1 lime, juiced

2 tbsp fresh coriander (cilantro) leaves, chopped

METHOD

1. Preheat the oven to 200°C (180°C fan) / 400F / gas 6. Brush the wonton wrappers with half of the vegetable oil, then drape them over the bars of a trivet set on a baking tray to make triangular pockets. Bake for 5 minutes or until crisp.

2. Heat the remaining vegetable oil in a wok and fry the garlic and ginger for 1 minute. Add the chicken and stir-fry for 3 minutes, then stir in the oyster sauce and sesame oil and cook for 1 minute. Leave to cool.

3. Mix the chicken with the onion, tomatoes and pepper, then stir in the lime juice and coriander and season to taste.

4. Fill the wonton pockets with the chicken mixture and serve immediately.

Beef with peppers and beans

SERVES: 4 | PREP TIME: 5 MINUTES | COOKING TIME: 10 MINUTES

INGREDIENTS

2 tbsp vegetable oil

1 tbsp fresh root ginger, finely chopped

3 cloves of garlic, finely chopped

spring onions (scallions), sliced diagonally, white and green parts separated

2 sirloin steaks, thinly sliced

150 g / 5 ½ oz / 1 cup green beans, cut into short lengths

1 yellow pepper, quartered and sliced

50 ml / 1 ¾ fl. oz / ¼ cup Shaoxing rice wine

75 ml / 2 ½ fl. oz / ¹/³ cup oyster sauce

METHOD

1. Heat the oil in a large wok and stir-fry the ginger, garlic and spring onion whites for 1 minute. Add the steak and stir-fry for 3 minutes.

2. Add the vegetables and stir-fry for 2 minutes. Add the rice wine and 50 ml of water, then cover the wok with a lid and steam for 2 minutes.

3. Stir in the oyster sauce and stir-fry for 2 minutes, then serve garnished with the spring onion greens.

43

Steak and peanut noodles

SERVES: 4 | PREP TIME: 3 HOURS | COOKING TIME: 15 MINUTES

INGREDIENTS

75 g / 2 ½ oz / ⅓ cup smooth peanut butter

1 tbsp runny honey

2 tbsp dark soy sauce

1 tsp Chinese five spice

1 clove of garlic, crushed

300 g / 10 ½ oz rump steak, thinly sliced

300 g / 10 ½ oz thin rice noodles

2 tbsp vegetable oil

2 red chillies (chilies), chopped

2 tsp fresh root ginger, finely chopped

200 g / 5 oz / 1 cup green beans, chopped

2 large carrots, shredded

1 litre / 1 pint 14 fl. oz / 4 cups beef stock

METHOD

1. Mix the peanut butter with the honey, soy sauce, five spice and garlic. Add the steak and stir well to coat, then marinate in the fridge for 3 hours.

2. Cook the noodles in boiling water according to the packet instructions or until al dente. Drain well, cover and set to one side.

3. Meanwhile, heat the oil in a wok and stir-fry the chillies and ginger for 1 minute. Add the beans and carrot, then stir-fry for 2 minutes.

4. Add the beef and marinade and stir-fry for 3 minutes or until just cooked. Add the stock and bring to a simmer, then toss together with the noodles and serve immediately.

44

Crispy sesame chicken

SERVES: 4 | PREP TIME: 15 MINUTES | COOKING TIME: 5 MINUTES

INGREDIENTS

vegetable oil, for deep frying

75 g / 2 ½ oz / ½ cup cornflour (cornstarch)

2 eggs, beaten

2 tsp sesame oil

100 g / 3 ½ oz / ⅔ cup panko breadcrumbs

30 g / 1 oz / ¼ cup sesame seeds

4 skinless chicken breasts, cut into strips

METHOD

1. Heat the oil in a deep fat fryer, according to the manufacturer's instructions, to a temperature of 180°C (350F).

2. Put the cornflour in a bowl and season with salt and pepper. Beat the eggs with the sesame oil in a second bowl and mix the panko crumbs and sesame seeds in a third.

3. Dip the chicken strips first in the cornflour, then in the egg, then in the breadcrumbs.

4. Fry the chicken in batches for 5 minutes or until crisp and golden brown and then transfer to a drain on plenty of kitchen paper.

Pork wontons

SERVES: 2-4 | PREP TIME: 25 MINUTES | COOKING TIME: 10 MINUTES

INGREDIENTS

vegetable oil, for deep frying

300 g / 10 ½ oz pork mince

1 clove of garlic, minced

15 g / ½ oz root ginger, grated

2 spring onions (scallions), sliced

1 tsp light soy sauce

1 tsp oyster sauce

1 tbsp coriander (cilantro), chopped

1 egg beaten

20 wonton wrappers

METHOD

1. Heat the oil in a deep fat fryer to 180°C / 350F. Alternatively heat enough oil in a wok to shallow fry.

2. Combine the pork, garlic, ginger, spring onions, soy sauce, oyster sauce and coriander in a bowl.

3. Add a splash of water to the beaten egg and place into a bowl.

4. To make the wontons, place a wrapper in your hand and place a teaspoon of the pork mixture into the centre of the wrapper. Using your fingertip, place egg wash about the edges of the wrapper and fold into a triangle, ensuring there are no air pockets, and seal. Repeat until all the mixture has been used.

5. Carefully place the wontons into the oil and cook for 1-2 minutes each until golden brown. Remove with a slotted spoon and drain onto kitchen paper.

Chicken and coconut soup

SERVES: 8 | PREP TIME: 15 MINUTES | COOKING TIME: 50 MINUTES

INGREDIENTS

1 kg whole small chicken

50 g / 1 ¾ oz / ⅓ cup fresh root ginger, sliced

5 cloves of garlic, squashed

6 spring onions (scallions), tied into a knot

2 leeks, sliced

800 ml / 1 pint 7 fl. oz / 3 ¼ cups canned coconut milk

1 small bunch fresh coriander (cilantro), chopped

½ tbsp caster (superfine) sugar

2 tbsp light soy sauce

1 lime, juiced

METHOD

1. Rub the chicken inside and out with 2 tsp of salt, then stuff the cavity with ginger, garlic and spring onions. Have a kettle of boiling water at the ready.

2. Put the leeks and coconut milk in a saucepan large enough to accommodate the chicken and bring to the boil. Carefully lower in the chicken, then add enough boiling water to cover the chicken by 2.5 cm (1 in).

3. When the liquid returns to the boil, lower the heat and simmer gently for 15 minutes. Turn off the hob, cover the pan and leave the chicken to cook in the residual heat for 30 minutes.

4. Carefully remove the chicken from the pan and discard the skin. Pull the meat off the carcass and cut it into bite-sized pieces, then return it to the saucepan.

5. Bring the soup to a gentle simmer and stir in half of the coriander. Season to taste with sugar, soy sauce and lime juice.

6. Ladle the soup into bowls and garnish with black pepper and the remaining coriander.

Chicken and egg noodle soup

SERVES: 4 | PREP TIME: 5 MINUTES | COOKING TIME: 10 MINUTES

●●●●●●●●●●●●●●●●●●●●●●●●●●

INGREDIENTS

400 g / 14 oz medium egg noodles

1 tbsp rice wine vinegar

4 very fresh eggs

1.2 litres / 2 pints / 4 ¾ cups pork or chicken stock

1 large chicken breast, sliced

12 baby sweetcorn, cut into bite-sized chunks

100 g / 3 ½ oz / 1 ½ cups oyster mushrooms, torn into bite-sized chunks if large

¼ Chinese cabbage, shredded

1 handful bean sprouts

2 spring onions (scallions), chopped, green parts only

1 tbsp chilli (chili) paste

METHOD

1. Cook the noodles in boiling water according to the packet instructions, then drain and divide between four warm bowls.

2. At the same time, bring a saucepan of water to a gentle simmer and stir in the vinegar. Poach the eggs gently for 3 minutes, then remove and transfer to a bowl of cold water.

3. Meanwhile, bring the stock to the boil in a separate saucepan. Add the chicken and sweetcorn and poach gently for 3 minutes. Add the mushrooms and cabbage and poach for 2 minutes. Add the bean sprouts and poach for 1 minute.

4. Divide the soup between the bowls and top each one with a poached egg, a sprinkle of spring onion greens and a little chilli paste.

Pork and bamboo shoot siu mai

MAKES: 24 | PREP TIME: 45 MINUTES | COOKING TIME: 10 MINUTES

INGREDIENTS

175 g / 6 oz / 1 ¼ cups plain (all-purpose) flour

225 g / 8 oz minced pork

2 spring onions (scallions), finely chopped

1 tsp fresh root ginger, finely grated

100 g / 3 ½ oz / ½ cup canned bamboo shoots, finely chopped

1 tbsp light soy sauce

1 tsp caster (superfine) sugar

1 tsp sesame oil

1 tsp cornflour (cornstarch)

1 egg white, beaten

2 tbsp crab roe (optional)

METHOD

1. Sift the flour into a bowl and stir in 160 ml of recently boiled water. Knead for 8 minutes to form a dough. Rest for 30 minutes.

2. Meanwhile, mix the pork with the spring onions, ginger, bamboo shoots, soy sauce, sugar, sesame oil and cornflour. Season.

3. Divide the dough into 24 balls, then roll out each one into a 7.5 cm (3 in) circle.

4. Put a heaped teaspoon of filling in the centre of each circle, then brush round the edge with egg white. Gather up the edges and twist to seal, leaving a small opening at the top. Add a small piece of crab roe to the top of each one, if using.

5. Space out in oiled steamer baskets and steam for 10 minutes, then serve immediately.

Barbecue pork

SERVES: 4-6 | PREP TIME: 4 HOURS | COOKING TIME: 20 MINUTES

INGREDIENTS

2 tbsp honey

1 tbsp oyster sauce

2 tbsp dark soy sauce

1 tbsp light soy sauce

2 tsp Chinese five spice

1 tbsp sesame oil

400 g / 14 oz pork tenderloin

rice and wilted greens to serve

METHOD

1. Combine the honey, oyster sauce, soy sauces, five spice and sesame oil in a pan. Heat gently and stir. Set aside to cool.

2. Coat the pork in the marinade and leave for 4 hours or overnight in the refrigerator.

3. When ready to cook, preheat the oven to 180°C (160°C fan) / 350F / gas 4 and allow the pork to come up to room temperature.

4. Line a baking tray with foil and place the pork on top, reserving the leftover marinade.

5. Roast in the oven for 18-20 minutes, basting during cooking.

6. Remove to rest for 10 minutes. Slice before serving with steamed rice and wilted greens.

Singapore noodles with chicken

SERVES: 4 | PREP TIME: 15 MINUTES | COOKING TIME: 10 MINUTES

INGREDIENTS

400 g / 14 oz thin rice noodles

2 tbsp vegetable oil

1 skinless chicken breast, cut into chunks

2 red chillies (chilies), sliced diagonally

¼ savoy cabbage, sliced

1 large carrot, peeled and coarsely grated

2 tbsp curry powder

50 ml / 1 ¾ fl. oz / ¼ cup Shaoxing rice wine

2 tbsp light soy sauce

1 tsp sesame oil

METHOD

1. Soak the noodles according to the packet instructions, then drain well.

2. Heat the oil in a large wok and fry the chicken until it begins to brown.

3. Add the chillies, cabbage and carrot and stir-fry for 2 minutes.

4. Add the noodles, then sprinkle the curry powder evenly over the top and toss well.

5. Add the rice wine, soy sauce and sesame oil and stir-fry for 1 minute, then divide between four warm bowls and serve immediately.

Omurice

SERVES: 1 | PREP TIME: 10 MINUTES | COOKING TIME: 20 MINUTES

INGREDIENTS

1 tsp vegetable oil

1 shallot, diced

1 clove of garlic, minced

1 tbsp ginger, minced

80 g / 2 ¾ oz chicken breast, diced

80 g / 2 ¾ oz cooked rice

2 tsp soy sauce

pinch of chilli (chili) flakes

2 spring onions (scallions), chopped

1 carrot, grated

1 tsp Sichuan pepper, ground

2 eggs beaten

1 tsp milk

1 tsp sesame oil

1 tbsp oyster sauce

1 tbsp mayonnaise

METHOD

1.   Heat the oil in a non-stick pan over a moderate heat. Add the shallot and fry for 1-2 minutes until softened. Add the garlic and ginger and fry for a further minute.

2.   Add the chicken breast to the pan and cook for 5-6 minutes until coloured all over.

3.   Add the cooked rice and stir to combine, then fry until the rice is warmed and started to colour.

4.   Mix through the soy, chilli, spring onions, carrot and pepper. Continue to cook until warmed and check the seasoning.

5.   Whisk together the eggs and milk. Heat the sesame oil in a separate pan and once hot, add the egg and spread evenly over the base of the pan to form an omelette.

6.   Spoon the chicken and rice into the centre of the omelette. Fold the edges over to encompass the filling.

7.   Carefully turn the omurice omelette onto a plate so that the folded edges are underneath. Drizzle over the oyster sauce and mayonnaise before serving.

Char siu buns

ERVES: 12 | PREP TIME: 2 HOURS, 45 MINUTES | COOKING TIME: 12 MINUTES

INGREDIENTS

300 g / 10 ½ oz / 2 cups plain (all-purpose) flour

150 g / 5 ½ oz / 1 cup cornflour (cornstarch)

75 g / 2 ½ oz / ⅓ cup caster (superfine) sugar

1 tsp easy blend dried yeast

65 ml / 2 ¼ fl. oz / ⅓ cup vegetable oil

2 shallots, finely chopped

1 tbsp muscovado sugar

2 tbsp dark soy sauce

1 tbsp oyster sauce

1 tbsp sesame oil

100 ml / 3 ½ fl. oz / ½ cup chicken stock

225 g / 8 oz Chinese roast pork, diced

2 ½ tsp baking powder

2 tbsp sesame seeds

1 red food colouring stamp (optional)

METHOD

1. Reserve 1 tablespoon of plain flour and mix the rest with the cornflour, caster sugar and yeast. Stir 50 ml of oil into 200 ml of warm water, then stir into the flour.

2. Knead the dough for 10 minutes, then cover and leave to rise for 2 hours.

3. Meanwhile, heat the remaining oil in a wok and fry the shallots for 2 minutes. Add the muscovado sugar, soy sauce, oyster sauce and sesame oil and bring to a simmer. Whisk in the reserved flour, then gradually incorporate the stock. When the mixture bubbles and thickens, stir in the diced pork and set aside to cool.

4. Knead the baking powder into the dough. Leave to rest for 15 minutes.

5. Divide the dough into twelve equal balls. Flatten each ball and add a spoonful of pork to the centre of each one. Gather up the edges and crimp to seal.

6. Sprinkle twelve squares of greaseproof paper with sesame seeds and place the buns on top, sealed side down. Steam the buns on the paper squares for 12 minutes, ensuring there's plenty of room for them to expand. Stamp the buns with red food colouring, if desired, then serve.

Chicken and noodles with oyster sauce

SERVES: 4 | PREP TIME: 10 MINUTES | COOKING TIME: 10 MINUTES

INGREDIENTS

300 g / 10 ½ oz wide wheat noodles

2 tbsp vegetable oil

2 cloves of garlic, thinly sliced

1 tbsp root ginger, thinly sliced

300 g / 10 ½ oz / 2 cups skinless boneless chicken thighs, sliced

1 large carrot, julienned

2 large mild red chillies (chilies), sliced diagonally

2 tbsp Shaoxing rice wine

50 ml / 1 ¾ fl. oz / ¼ cup oyster sauce

2 tsp sesame oil

1 handful fresh coriander (cilantro), chopped

METHOD

1. Cook the noodles in boiling water according to the packet instructions or until al dente, then drain well.

2. Heat the oil in a large wok and fry the garlic and ginger for 2 minutes.

3. Add the chicken and stir-fry for 3 minutes or until lightly coloured. Add the carrot and chillies and stir-fry for 2 minutes.

4. Add the rice wine, oyster sauce and sesame oil and stir well. Add the noodles and stir-fry for 2 more minutes. Serve immediately, garnished with coriander.

Duck pancakes

MAKES: 16 | PREP TIME: 1 HOUR 30 MINUTES | COOKING TIME: 3 MINUTES

INGREDIENTS

350 g / 12 ½ z / 1 ½ cups plain (all-purpose) flour

1 tsp sesame oil

TO SERVE:

100 ml / 3 ½ fl. oz / ½ cup hoisin sauce

½ Cantonese roast duck,
boned and sliced (see recipe in Meat Dishes)

1 small cucumber, julienned

3 spring onions (scallions), julienned

METHOD

1. Mix the flour with ½ teaspoon of salt in a bowl. Stir in 150 ml boiling water, adding a little more if needed to form a soft dough. When it has cooled down enough to handle, knead for 5 minutes, then cover and leave to rest for 1 hour.

2. Divide the dough into sixteen balls and flatten them slightly. Brush the top of the discs with sesame oil and sandwich them together with the oiled sides touching. Roll out the discs on a lightly floured surface into 7.5 cm (3 in) circles.

3. Heat a frying pan over a medium heat without any oil. Fry one of the pancakes for 30 seconds or until it starts to puff slightly. Flip it over and cook the other side until lightly coloured in places. Peel the pancake apart and transfer to a covered steamer basket. Repeat with the rest of the pancakes.

4. When you're ready to serve, steam the pancakes for 2 minutes.

5. Take them to the table with the accompaniments and top the pancakes with a smear of hoisin, a few slices of duck and some cucumber and spring onion.

Pork bao bun

SERVES: 2-4 | PREP TIME: 2 HOURS | COOKING TIME: 20 MINUTES

INGREDIENTS

1 tsp fast acting yeast

250 g / 9 oz / 1 ⅔ cups strong white bread flour

25 g / 1 oz caster (superfine) sugar

1 tsp salt

4 pork loin steaks

2 tbsp soy sauce

1 tsp honey

1 lime, juiced

1 tbsp sesame oil

2 carrots, shredded

½ cucumber, sliced

2 red chillies (chili), sliced

handful of coriander (cilantro), chopped

2 tbsp oyster sauce

METHOD

1. Add the yeast to a jug of 125ml warm water, cover and leave for 2-3 minutes to activate.

2. Combine the flour, sugar and salt in a bowl. Pour in the water and mix to combine, adding a little more water if too dry. Turn out onto a floured surface and knead for 10 minutes, then cover with a damp tea towel and leave in a warm place to prove for 1 hour.

3. Cut sheets of greaseproof paper into squares roughly 20 cm (8 in) square.

4. Knock back the dough and divide into six equal sized balls. Roll out into oval shapes to fit the squares of greaseproof paper. Place onto a square of paper before placing another on top, then fold to sandwich the paper. Place onto a tray and cover with cling film, leave to prove again for 30 minutes.

5. Preheat the oven to 180°C (160°C fan) / 350F / gas 4. Combine the pork with the soy, honey, lime and sesame oil. Place into the oven and cook for 18-20 minutes until slightly charred and cooked through.

6. Place a steamer on the heat and steam the buns for 8-10 minutes until puffy and cooked through. Remove from the steamer and remove the paper. Fill the buns with the charred pork, carrot, cucumber, chilli and coriander, and top with the oyster sauce.

Tea eggs with soba noodles

RVES: 4 | PREP TIME: 3 HOURS, 30 MINUTES | COOKING TIME: 15 MINUTES

INGREDIENTS

4 large eggs

2 tbsp loose leaf tea

1 tbsp Chinese five spice

1 tbsp brown sugar

2 tbsp soy sauce

1 tsp sesame oil

400 g / 14 oz soba (buckwheat) noodles

2 tbsp vegetable oil

neless chicken thighs, cubed, with skin left on

2 cloves of garlic, crushed

2 tsp fresh root ginger, finely grated

½ carrot, julienned

) g / 5 ½ oz / 2 cups mushrooms, thickly sliced

75 ml / 2 ½ fl. oz / ⅓ cup oyster sauce

2 tbsp large peanuts

METHOD

1. Boil the eggs for 8 minutes, then plunge into iced water and leave to cool for 5 minutes. Drain the eggs, then tap them all over with a teaspoon to crack the shell, being careful not to puncture the membrane underneath.

2. Measure the tea, five spice, sugar and soy sauce into the saucepan. Add the eggs with enough cold water to just cover them. Cover and simmer very gently for 1 hour, then turn off the heat and leave to cool for 2 hours. Peel the eggs, rub with sesame oil and set aside.

3. Cook the noodles according to the packet instructions, then drain and plunge into iced water. Drain well.

4. Meanwhile, heat the oil in a large wok and fry the chicken skin side down for 4 minutes. Add the garlic and ginger and stir-fry for 2 minutes. Add the carrot and mushrooms and stir-fry for 4 minutes.

5. Add the oyster sauce, peanuts and 50 ml of water. When it starts to simmer, add the noodles and warm through.

6. Divide the noodles between four warm plates and top each one with a tea egg.

Mongolian beef

SERVES: 4 | PREP TIME: **10 MINUTES** | COOKING TIME: **10 MINUTES**

INGREDIENTS

2 tsp cornflour (cornstarch)

1 tbsp Shaoxing rice wine

1 tbsp dark soy sauce

450 g / 1 lb fillet steak, thinly sliced

50 ml / 1 ¾ fl. oz / ¼ cup vegetable oil

3 clove of garlic, finely chopped

1 ½ tbsp fresh root ginger, finely julienned

6 spring onions (scallions), whites quartered
lengthways, greens cut into short lengths

50 ml / 1 ¾ fl. oz / ¼ cup oyster sauce

2 tbsp runny honey

2 tbsp light soy sauce

½ tsp sesame oil

crispy rice noodles, to serve

METHOD

1. Slake the cornflour with 2 tbsp of water, then
    stir in the rice wine and dark soy. Toss the
    steak with the mixture, then cover and
    marinate in the fridge for 1 hour.

2. Heat 2 tbsp of the vegetable oil in a large wok
    until smoking hot. Stir-fry the beef for
    3 minutes or until sealed and lightly
    coloured. Transfer to a bowl and set aside,
    then clean the wok.

3. Heat the rest of the vegetable oil in the wok
    and fry the garlic and ginger for 1 minute.
    Add the spring onions and stir-fry for
    2 minutes.

4. Return the beef to the wok, then add the
    oyster sauce, honey and light soy sauce.
    Stir-fry for 2 minutes, then stir in the sesame
    oil and taste the sauce for seasoning.

5. Serve immediately on a bed of
    crispy rice noodles.

Crispy fried pork

SERVES: 2 | PREP TIME: 4 MINUTES | COOKING TIME: 45 MINUTES

INGREDIENTS

1 tbsp Chinese five spice

1 tbsp salt

1 tbsp Sichuan pepper, ground

400 g / 14 oz pork belly slices, cubed

1 tsp vegetable oil

METHOD

1. Combine the five spice, salt and pepper. Add to the pork belly and toss to coat, then place onto a baking tray and leave for up to 4 hours.

2. Preheat the oven to 200°C (180°C fan) / 400F / gas 6.

3. Place the pork into the oven and roast for 40 minutes. Remove from the oven and set aside.

4. When ready to serve, heat the oil in a wok or frying pan over a medium high heat. Add the pork and stir-fry until crisp.

5. Serve the crispy pork with sticky rice or wilted vegetables.

Chicken noodle stir-fry

SERVES: 4 | PREP TIME: 10 MINUTES | COOKING TIME: 10 MINUTES

INGREDIENTS

200 g / 7 oz wide flat rice noodles

2 tbsp vegetable oil

2 cloves of garlic, thinly sliced

1 tbsp fresh root ginger, thinly sliced

spring onions (scallions), whites chopped, greens
cut into short lengths

2 skinless chicken breasts, sliced

1 large carrot, julienned with a mandolin

¼ Chinese cabbage, thinly sliced

2 tbsp light soy sauce

METHOD

1. Cook the noodles in boiling water according
    to the packet instructions or until al dente,
    then drain well.

2. Heat the oil in a large wok and fry the garlic,
    ginger and spring onion whites for
    2 minutes.

3. Add the chicken and stir-fry for 3 minutes or
    until lightly coloured. Add the carrots and
    cabbage and stir-fry for 2 minutes.

4. Add the soy sauce, noodles and spring onion
    greens and stir-fry for 2 more minutes, then
    taste and adjust the seasoning with a little
    more soy sauce if needed.

5. Serve immediately.

69

Spicy chicken noodle soup

SERVES: 4 | PREP TIME: 5 MINUTES | COOKING TIME: 15 MINUTES

INGREDIENTS

300 g / 10 ½ oz thin egg noodles

1 litre / 1 pint 14 fl. oz / 4 cups clear light chicken stock

2 tbsp Shaoxing rice wine

1 tsp caster (superfine) sugar

1 red chilli (chili), sliced

1 green chilli (chili), sliced

2 skinless chicken breasts, cut into bite-sized chunks

1 handful coriander (cilantro) leaves

METHOD

1. Cook the noodles in boiling water according to the packet instructions or until al dente. Plunge into cold water, then drain well.

2. Heat the stock in a saucepan with the rice wine, sugar and chillies. When it starts to boil, add the chicken and simmer very gently for 4 minutes or until just cooked through.

3. Add the noodles to the broth and warm through, then season to taste with salt.

4. Divide the soup between four bowls and serve garnished with coriander leaves.

Spare ribs

SERVES: 6 | PREP TIME: 4 HOURS 15 MINUTES | COOKING TIME: 6 MINUTES

INGREDIENTS

1 ½ tbsp red fermented bean curd

2 tbsp Shaoxing rice wine

1 tbsp light soy sauce

1 tbsp runny honey

1 tsp Chinese five spice

1 tsp garlic powder

½ tsp ground white pepper

900 g / 2 lb small ribs, separated

vegetable oil, for deep-frying

2 tbsp cornflour (cornstarch)

2 tbsp plain (all-purpose) flour

1 tbsp sesame seeds, toasted

METHOD

1. Mash the bean curd into the rice wine, then whisk in the soy sauce, honey, five spice, garlic and white pepper. Add the ribs and toss well to coat. Leave to marinate in the fridge for 4 hours.

2. Heat the oil in a deep fat fryer, according to the manufacturer's instructions, to a temperature of 180°C (350F).

3. Sprinkle the cornflour and plain flour over the ribs and toss well to coat.

4. Deep fry the ribs in batches of six for 6 minutes or until deep golden brown and cooked through. Drain on plenty of kitchen paper. Sprinkle the ribs with sesame seeds and serve immediately.

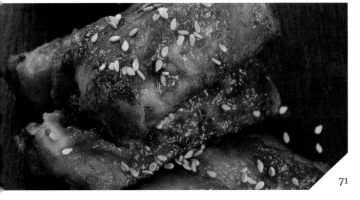

Korean style noodle soup

SERVES: 2-4 | PREP TIME: 15 MINUTES | COOKING TIME: 20 MINUTES

INGREDIENTS

1 tsp vegetable oil

300 g / 10 ½ oz pork mince

750 ml / 25 fl. oz / 3 cups chicken stock

1 inch piece of root ginger, grated

2 cloves of garlic, sliced

1 tbsp Korean chilli (chili) powder

1 tbsp sesame oil

1 tbsp fish sauce

2 limes, juiced

300 g / 10 ½ oz egg noodles

200 g / 7 oz bean sprouts

2 carrots, julienned

2 spring onions (scallions), sliced

METHOD

1. Heat the oil in a saucepan and fry off the pork mince until browned and starting to colour.

2. Pour the stock into the saucepan and add the ginger, garlic, chilli powder, sesame, fish sauce and lime juice. Heat until boiling before turning down to a simmer and covering. Leave for 8-10 minutes.

3. Cook the noodles as per the packet instructions, drain and divide between serving bowls. Add the bean sprouts and carrots to the soup and continue to cook for a further 5 minutes. Spoon the soup over the noodles and garnish with the spring onions.

Beef and prawn noodles

SERVES: 2 | PREP TIME: 15 MINUTES | COOKING TIME: 20 MINUTES

INGREDIENTS

220 g / 8 oz egg noodles

250 g / 9 oz beef steak, sliced

2 tsp soy sauce

1 tsp Chinese five spice

1 tsp vegetable oil

2 cloves of garlic, chopped

1 chilli (chili), chopped

120 g / 4 ¼ oz king prawns, deshelled

2 carrots, julienned

handful of coriander (cilantro), chopped

METHOD

1.   Cook the noodles as per the packet instructions. Drain and set aside until needed.

2.   Combine the beef, soy and five spice in a bowl.

3.   Heat the oil in a wok over a moderate heat. Add the garlic and chilli and fry for 30 seconds until fragrant. Pour the beef and soy into the wok and stir-fry for 2-3 minutes until the meat has browned.

4.   Add the prawns to the pan and continue to stir-fry until the prawns are pink and firm.

5.   Add the noodles and carrots to the pan and toss to coat with the juices from the pan.

6.   Divide between two serving plates and garnish with the chopped coriander.

73

Bak kut teh

SERVES: 2-4 | PREP TIME: 10 MINUTES | COOKING TIME: 1 HOUR 15 MINUTE

INGREDIENTS

400 g / 14 oz pork ribs

2 tbsp Sichuan peppercorns

1 tbsp salt

1 tsp brown sugar

4 cloves of garlic, bruised

1 cinnamon stick

1 star anise

2 tsp cloves

2 tbsp dark soy sauce

1 tbsp oyster sauce

1 tbsp rice vinegar

250 g / 9 oz shiitake mushrooms, sliced

200 g / 7 oz pak choi, leaves separated

METHOD

1. Cut the ribs into small pieces and place into a large pan and cover with cold water.

2. Heat the water until simmering, skimming off any scum that collects on the surface. Continue to do this until the soup is clear.

3. Add the pepper, salt, sugar, garlic, cinnamon, star anise, cloves, soy, oyster sauce and vinegar. Cover and simmer for 1 hour until fragrant and the pork has softened.

4. Add the mushrooms and pok choi to the pan and continue to cook for a further 12-15 minutes.

5. Check seasoning before serving with sticky rice.

Braised duck with noodles

SERVES: 6 | PREP TIME: 15 MINUTES | COOKING TIME: 1 HOUR, 10 MINUTES

INGREDIENTS

1.8 kg / 4 lb whole duck

75 ml / 2 ½ fl. oz / ⅓ cup dark soy sauce

2 tbsp Shaoxing rice wine

1 tsp caster (superfine) sugar

2 stalks lemongrass, bruised

4 slices fresh root ginger

4 spring onions (scallions), chopped,
green and white parts separated

2 star anise

2 cloves of garlic, squashed

400 g / 14 oz vermicelli rice noodles

0 g / 5 ½ oz / 4 ½ cups ong choi (water spinach)

METHOD

1. Rub the duck inside and out with 1 tablespoon of salt. Put the soy sauce, rice wine, sugar, lemongrass, ginger, spring onion whites, star anise and garlic in a saucepan large enough to accommodate the duck. Stir in 750 ml of water.

2. Bring to the boil, then carefully lower in the duck, breast side down. Cover and simmer gently for 30 minutes, adding a little boiling water if the liquid level falls below halfway up the duck.

3. Turn the duck over, then cover and simmer for 30 minutes or until the meat pulls easily away from the bones.

4. Cook the noodles in boiling water according to the packet instructions or until al dente. Drain well and divide between six bowls.

5. Carefully transfer the duck to a carving board and scoop out and discard the flavourings from the broth. Add the ong choi to the broth and simmer for 5 minutes while you carve the duck.

6. Divide the duck and ong choi between the bowls. Taste the broth and either season with salt or dilute with a little water if too strong. Ladle a little into each bowl and serve, garnished with spring onion greens.

Grilled chicken with noodles

SERVES: 4 | PREP TIME: 1 HOUR 10 MINUTES | COOKING TIME: 8 MINU~

INGREDIENTS

2 large skinless chicken breasts

2 tbsp light soy sauce

1 tbsp runny honey

1 tsp Chinese five spice

1 lime, juiced

400 g / 14 oz thin egg noodles

2 tbsp sunflower oil

2 cloves of garlic, sliced

2 tsp fresh root ginger, finely chopped

4 spring onions (scallions), chopped,
green and white parts separated

2 mild red chillies (chilies), sliced

3 mixed peppers, thinly sliced

1 carrot, julienned

1 tsp sesame oil

coriander (cilantro) leaves, to garnish

METHOD

1. Put the chicken in a freezer bag with the soy
honey, five spice and lime juice. Massage to
coat, then marinate in the fridge for 1 hour.

2. Cook the noodles according to packet
instructions, then drain and plunge into
iced water. Drain well.

3. Cook the chicken under a hot grill for
4 minutes on each side, or until only just
cooked in the centre. Meanwhile, heat the o~
in a large wok and fry the garlic, ginger,
spring onion whites and chillies
for 2 minutes.

4. Add the peppers and carrot and stir-fry for
minutes, then pour in the marinade from th~
freezer bag. As soon as it starts to bubble,
add the noodles and sesame oil and heat
through. Divide the noodles between four
warm bowls and garnish with spring onion
greens and coriander.

5. Slice the chicken and divide between
the bowls. Serve immediately.

Spinach jiaozi with pork

SERVES: 2-4 | PREP TIME: 1 HOUR | COOKING TIME: 10 MINUTES

INGREDIENTS

00 g / 3 ½ oz / ⅔ cups plain (all-purpose) flour

25 g / 1 oz spinach purée

50 ml / 1 ¾ fl. oz / ¼ cup hot water

½ tsp salt

250 g / 9 oz pork mince

2 cloves of garlic, minced

1 tbsp ginger, grated

2 spring onions (scallions), sliced

1 tsp chive, chopped

1 tsp soy sauce

1 tsp rice vinegar

g / 2 ¾ oz shiitake mushrooms, finely chopped

1 tbsp Sichuan pepper, ground

METHOD

1. Combine the flour, spinach, water and salt in a bowl and bring together with a wooden spoon. Add more water if a little dry.

2. Turn out onto a floured surface and knead the dough for 4-5 minutes until smooth and elastic. Roll into a ball and wrap in cling film, then leave to rest for up to an hour.

3. Place the remaining ingredients in a mixing bowl and mix to combine thoroughly.

4. Divide the dough in half and roll out to a sausage roughly 1 inch thick on a floured surface. Slice the dough at roughly 1 inch intervals and flatten with the palm of your hand. Roll to a rough circle shape as thinly as possible.

5. Place roughly 1 tablespoon of filling into the centre of the wrapper and fold into a semi-circle, making sure not to trap any air. Bring the two ends together to form a circular shape.

6. The dumpling can either be steamed in a steamer for 8-10 minutes, or fried in a pan. To fry place into a pan with a lid with some oil. Heat over a moderate heat and once the bottoms are crisp pour in a little water and place the lid on top. Leave to steam for 5-6 minutes.

Chicken and mushroom wui fan

SERVES: 4 | PREP TIME: 35 MINUTES | COOKING TIME: 8 MINUTES

INGREDIENTS

3 skinless chicken breasts, cut into
bite-sized chunks

150 g / 5 ½ oz / 1 ½ cup king oyster mushrooms,
chopped if large

2 tbsp light soy sauce

2 tsp sesame oil

2 tsp cornflour (cornstarch)

½ tsp ground white pepper

2 tbsp vegetable oil

2 cloves of garlic, finely chopped

½ tbsp root ginger, finely chopped

4 spring onions (scallions), chopped,
green and white parts separated

250 ml / 9 fl. oz / 1 cup chicken stock

2 tbsp oyster sauce

1 medium egg, beaten

450 g / 1 lb / 2 ½ cups freshly cooked long-grain rice

1 handful fresh coriander (cilantro) leaves

METHOD

1. Marinate the chicken and mushrooms in half the soy sauce, half the sesame oil, half the cornflour and the white pepper for 30 minutes.

2. Heat the vegetable oil in a wok and fry the garlic, ginger and spring onion whites for 1 minute. Add the chicken and mushrooms and stir-fry for 2 minutes. Add the stock and oyster sauce and bring to a simmer. Cook for 2 minutes.

3. Move the chicken and mushrooms to the side of the wok. Slake the remaining cornflour with the rest of the soy sauce and whisk it into the sauce. When it thickens, whisk in the egg, then fold in the rice.

4. Divide the mixture between four bowls and top with spring onion greens and coriander leaves.

Crispy sesame chicken noodle salad

SERVES: 4 | PREP TIME: 25 MINUTES | COOKING TIME: 2 MINUTES

INGREDIENTS

30 g / 1 oz / ½ cup dried wood ear fungus

400 g / 14 oz wide flat rice noodles

1 carrot, julienned

1 yellow pepper, deseeded and julienned

1 leek, sliced

150 g / 5 ½ oz / 1 cup sugar snap peas

75 g / 2 ½ oz / ½ cup peas

1 tbsp caster (superfine) sugar

1 lime, juiced, plus extra wedges to serve

1 tbsp fish sauce

2 tbsp spring onion (scallion)

1 red chilli (chili), sliced

300 g / 10 ½ oz / 2 cups crispy sesame chicken

1 tbsp sesame seeds

METHOD

1. Soak the fungus in cold water for 20 minutes, then drain well.

2. Meanwhile, cook the noodles according to the packet instructions, then drain and plunge into iced water. Drain well.

3. Blanch the vegetables in boiling salted water for 2 minutes, then drain and plunge into iced water. Drain well.

4. Divide the noodles, fungus and vegetables between four bowls.

5. Stir the sugar into the lime juice and fish sauce until it dissolves, then drizzle it over the salads and scatter with spring onion greens and chillies. Arrange the chicken on top and sprinkle with sesame seeds.

Sweet and sour pork

SERVES: 2 | PREP TIME: 15 MINUTES | COOKING TIME: 30 MINUTES

INGREDIENTS

1 tbsp rice wine vinegar

2 tbsp tomato purée

1 tsp soy sauce

200 ml / 7 fl. oz / ¾ cup pineapple juice

1 tsp soft brown sugar

1 tbsp vegetable oil

1 onion, sliced

2 red peppers, sliced

2 carrots, diced

250 g / 9 oz pork, sliced

120 g / 4 ¼ oz egg noodles

2 tsp cornflour (cornstarch)

METHOD

1. Combine the vinegar, tomato purée, soy, pineapple juice and sugar and whisk.

2. Heat the oil in a wok or frying pan over a medium high heat. Add the onion, peppers and carrots and fry for 6-8 minutes until softened. Remove and set aside.

3. Place the pork in the pan and stir-fry for 4-5 minutes until browned. Return the vegetables to the pan before pouring over the liquid. Allow to bubble gently for 12-15 minutes.

4. Cook the noodles in a pan of boiling water as per instructions, then drain and set aside.

5. Mix the cornflour with a little water to form a paste. Mix through the pork and vegetables to thicken the sauce. Serve the pork with the cooked noodles in bowls.

Duck in orange sauce

SERVES: 2-4 | PREP TIME: 10 MINUTES | COOKING TIME: 20 MINUTES

INGREDIENTS

3 duck breasts

2 tbsp Sichuan pepper

1 tsp vegetable oil

2 oranges, juiced

2 star anise

1 clove of garlic, minced

1 inch piece of root ginger, grated

2 tbsp light soy sauce

a handful of coriander (cilantro), chopped

METHOD

1. Preheat the oven to 180°C (160°C fan) / 350F / gas 4.

2. Score the skin of the duck and season.

3. Heat the oil in a frying pan over a medium high heat. Once the oil is smoking a little add the duck breasts skin-side down. Fry for 5 minutes before flipping over and cooking for a further 2-3 minutes.

4. Place into an ovenproof dish and roast in the oven for a further 8-10 minutes. Remove and set aside to rest. As the duck rests, place the orange juice, star anise, garlic, ginger and soy into a saucepan and gently simmer.

5. Pour the sauce over the duck and scatter with the chopped coriander. Serve with wilted Chinese greens and rice.

Deep fried pork with rice

SERVES: 2 | PREP TIME: 25 MINUTES | COOKING TIME: 25 MINUTES

INGREDIENTS

120 g / 4 ¼ oz / ⅔ cup long-grain rice

300 g / 10 ½ oz pork shoulder, diced

1 tsp soy sauce

1 tsp Chinese five spice

1 tsp garlic powder

1 tsp sesame oil

2 tbsp cornflour (cornstarch)

2 tbsp plain (all-purpose) flour

½ tsp white pepper

1 egg beaten

oil for frying

2 tsp black sesame seeds

METHOD

1. Cook the rice as per the packet instructions, then drain and set aside until needed.

2. Combine the pork with the soy, five spice, garlic powder and sesame oil. Leave for 15 minutes to combine. Meanwhile, heat the oil to about 180°C / 350F.

3. Mix the cornflour and plain flour together with the pepper and a pinch of salt. Dredge the pork in the flour before coating in the egg and dredging a second time in the flour.

4. Fry the pork in the oil for 3-5 minutes until crispy. Just before serving fry for a second time for a further 2-3 minutes until golden.

5. Serve the pork with the rice and sprinkle over the sesame seeds.

87

Pork ramen

SERVES: 4 | PREP TIME: 15 MINUTES | COOKING TIME: 30 MINUTES

INGREDIENTS

2 tbsp peanut oil

4 spring onions (scallions), sliced

2 cloves of garlic, minced

1 in piece of root ginger, grated

1 l / 35 fl. oz / 4 cups pork stock

2 tsp soy sauce

2 tsp fish sauce

4 pork medallions

1 tsp garlic powder

1 tsp Chinese five spice

180 g / 6 oz ramen noodles

handful of chives, chopped, to garnish

METHOD

1. Heat half the peanut oil in a saucepan. Add the spring onions, garlic and ginger and fry for 1-2 minutes until fragrant. Add the stock and bring to a boil. Reduce to a high simmer and cook for 12-15 minutes with the lid on.

2. Add the soy and fish sauce and continue to cool for a further 8-10 minutes. Season to taste, adding more soy if necessary.

3. Heat the remaining oil in a pan. Coat the pork with the garlic powder and five spice and cook in the pan for 8-10 minutes, turning once. Remove to rest and slice.

4. Cook the noodles as per the packet instructions, drain and divide between serving bowls. Pour over the soup before topping with the sliced pork and garnish.

Breaded chicken with pineapple

SERVES: 4 | PREP TIME: 20 MINUTES | COOKING TIME: 6 MINUTES

INGREDIENTS

tbsp vegetable oil, plus extra for deep-frying

1 red chilli (chili), chopped

2 cloves of garlic, finely chopped

2 tsp fresh root ginger, finely chopped

5 g / 8 oz / 1 small can pineapple chunks in juice

2 tbsp rice wine vinegar

2 tbsp light brown sugar

1 tbsp soy sauce

1 tsp cornflour (cornstarch)

75 g / 2 ½ oz / ½ cup plain (all-purpose) flour

2 eggs, beaten

100 g / 3 ½ oz / 1 cup panko breadcrumbs

4 small skinless chicken breasts

steamed rice, to serve

2 tbsp fresh coriander (cilantro), chopped

METHOD

1. Heat the vegetable oil in a wok and fry the chilli, garlic and ginger for 1 minute. Add the pineapple chunks and their juice, plus the vinegar, sugar and soy sauce.

2. When the sauce starts to simmer, slake the cornflour with 2 tablespoons of cold water, then stir it into the wok. Continue to stir over a medium heat until the sauce simmers and thickens. Heat the oil in a deep fat fryer to a temperature of 180°C (350F).

3. Put the flour, egg and breadcrumbs in three separate bowls and dip the chicken breasts alternately in each one. Deep-fry the chicken in two batches for 6 minutes or until nicely browned and cooked through.

4. Drain the chicken on plenty of kitchen paper and serve on a bed of rice with the pineapple sauce spooned over. Garnish with coriander.

Pork noodle soup

SERVES: 2 | PREP TIME: 1 HOUR | COOKING TIME: 30 MINUTES

INGREDIENTS

2 tsp honey

1 tsp oyster sauce

2 tsp dark soy sauce

1 tsp light soy sauce

1 tsp Chinese five spice

1 tbsp sesame oil

300 g / 10 ½ oz pork loin steaks

500 ml / 17 fl. oz / 2 cups chicken stock

15 g / ½ oz ginger, sliced

2 cloves of garlic, sliced

1 star anise

½ cinnamon stick

1 tsp chilli (chili) flakes

200 g / 7 oz egg noodles

100 g / 3 ½ oz bean sprouts

100 g / 3 ½ oz green (string) beans, sliced

25 g / 1 oz / ¼ cups cashew nuts, chopped

METHOD

1. Mix the honey, oyster sauce, soy sauces, five spice and sesame oil in a pan. Heat gently and stir to combine, this should only take a minute. Set aside to cool. Coat the pork in the marinade and leave for at least 1 hour.

2. Preheat the oven to 180°C (160°C fan) / 350F / gas. Place the pork onto a baking tray lined with foil. Roast in the oven for 18-20 minutes, basting at least once with the leftover marinade. Remove to rest before slicing.

3. Place the stock into a saucepan with the ginger, garlic, star anise, cinnamon and chilli. Heat until boiling before turning down to a simmer. Cover and cook for 10 minutes to let the flavours infuse, add dumplings if preferred.

4. Cook the noodles as per the packet instructions, drain and set aside.

5. Add the bean sprouts and beans to the pan and allow to cook for 10 minutes until softened. Divide the noodles between serving plates and top with the pork and soup before garnishing with the nuts.

Steamed pork belly buns

SERVES: 12 | PREP TIME: 2 HOURS, 45 MINUTES | COOKING TIME: 5 MINUTES

INGREDIENTS

450 g / 1 lb / 3 cups plain (all-purpose) flour

50 g / 1 ¾ oz / ¼ cup caster
(superfine) sugar

2 tbsp dried skimmed milk powder

½ tsp easy blend dried yeast

450 g / 1 lb / 3 cups pork belly, cubed

2 tbsp vegetable oil

1 tbsp runny honey

3 tbsp Shaoxing rice wine

1 tbsp light soy sauce

½ tbsp dark soy sauce

1 tbsp baking powder

2 tbsp sesame oil

shredded mooli (daikon), to serve

chopped spring onions (scallions) and coriander
(cilantro), to garnish

METHOD

1. Mix the flour with the sugar, milk powder
   and yeast. Stir in enough warm water to
   form a soft dough (around 250 ml).

2. Knead the dough for 10 minutes,
   then cover and leave to rise for 2 hours.
   Meanwhile, blanch the pork for 2 minutes in
   boiling water. Drain and dry.

3. Heat the oil in a wok, add the pork and
   stir-fry for 4 minutes. Drizzle with honey
   and stir-fry until browned. Add the rice
   wine, soy sauces and 500 ml of water, then
   simmer gently for 1 hour, stirring
   occasionally. Increase the heat and boil until
   reduced to a thick sauce. Keep warm.

4. When the dough has risen, knead in the
   baking powder and leave to rest
   for 15 minutes.

5. Divide the dough into twelve equal balls.
   Flatten each ball, brush with sesame oil and
   fold in half. Leave each one to rise on a square
   of oiled greaseproof paper for 30 minutes.

6. Steam the buns on the paper squares for
   5 minutes, leaving plenty of room to expand.
   Unfold the buns and fill with shredded
   mooli and pork belly, then garnish with
   spring onion and coriander.

Pork and courgette jiaozi

MAKES: 32 | PREP TIME: 1 HOUR | COOKING TIME: 10 MINUTES

INGREDIENTS

175 g / 6 oz / 1 ¼ cups plain (all-purpose) flour

225 g / 8 oz minced pork

2 tbsp dark soy sauce

1 tbsp Shaoxing rice wine

1 tsp sesame oil

1 egg, separated

225 g / 8 oz / 1 ¾ cups courgette (zucchini), coarsely grated

100 g / 3 ½ oz / 2 cups chives, finely chopped, plus extra to garnish

½ tbsp fresh root ginger, finely grated

1 tbsp vegetable oil

3 clove of garlic, finely chopped

1 tbsp light soy sauce

METHOD

1. Stir 160 ml of recently boiled water into the flour, then knead for 8 minutes. Rest for 30 minutes.

2. Meanwhile, mix the pork with 50 ml cold water, then beat in the dark soy, rice wine, sesame oil and egg yolk. Stir in the courgette, chives and ginger.

3. Roll the dough into thirty 7.5 cm (3 in) circles. Lay one circle on a dumpling press and add a heaped teaspoon of filling. Brush the edges with egg white, then fold in half and squeeze to seal. Repeat to make 32.

4. Boil a large saucepan of water. Add half of the dumplings and stir well. Cover and return to the boil, then add 250 ml of cold water. Repeat twice more, then remove the dumplings from the pan with a slotted spoon. Repeat the process with the rest of the dumplings.

5. Heat the vegetable oil and fry the garlic for 1 minute, then stir in the soy sauce. Divide the dumplings between warm plates and top with the fried garlic and a sprinkle of chives.

95

Spicy pork noodles

SERVES: 4 | PREP TIME: 10 MINUTES + OVERNIGHT | COOKING TIME: 10 MINUTE

INGREDIENTS

2 tbsp hoisin sauce

2 tbsp sweet soy sauce or kecap manis

2 tbsp runny honey

1 tsp Chinese five spice

1 tsp sesame oil

450 g / 1 lb pork loin, cubed

400 g / 14 oz medium egg noodles

2 tbsp vegetable oil

2 cloves of garlic, crushed

2 tsp fresh root ginger, finely grated

1 red onion, thinly sliced

1 carrot, julienned

2 spring onions (scallions), julienned

METHOD

1. Put the hoisin, soy, honey, five spice and sesame oil in a saucepan. Stir continuously while it comes to the boil, then leave to cool. Scrape the mixture into a freezer bag, add the pork and massage well to coat. Marinate in the fridge overnight.

2. Cook the noodles according to the packet instructions, then drain and plunge into iced water. Drain well.

3. Remove the pork from the freezer bag and reserve the marinade.

4. Heat the vegetable oil in a wok and fry the garlic and ginger for 30 seconds. Add the onion and stir-fry for 1 minute.

5. Add the pork and stir-fry for 4 minutes or until lightly coloured. Add the carrot and noodles and stir-fry for 2 minutes. Pour in the reserved marinade, then cover and cook for 2 minutes.

6. Toss in the spring onions, then divide between four warm plates and serve immediately.

96

Braised brisket noodle soup

RVES: 4 | PREP TIME: 20 MINUTES | COOKING TIME: 3 HOURS, 15 MINUTES

INGREDIENTS

1 tbsp vegetable oil

600 g / 1 lb 5 ½ oz beef brisket, in one piece

4 large shallots, unpeeled

25 g / 1 oz fresh root ginger, in one piece

1 carrot, cut into large chunks

8 cloves

1 tbsp white peppercorns

2 star anise

1 tbsp caster (superfine) sugar

50 ml / 1 ¾ fl. oz / ¼ cup fish sauce

300 g / 10 ½ oz glass noodles

150 g / 5 ½ oz / 1 ½ cup shimeji mushrooms

4 baby pak choi, leaves separated

1 red chilli (chili), sliced

METHOD

1. Heat the vegetable oil in a frying pan and sear the beef until browned. Meanwhile, toast the shallots, ginger and carrot under a hot grill until dark brown all over.

2. Transfer the beef and toasted vegetables to a large saucepan and add the cloves, peppercorns, star anise, sugar and fish sauce. Pour over 1.5 litres of water.

3. Bring to the boil, then cover and simmer gently for 3 hours or until the beef is tender. Transfer the beef to a carving board and cover with a double layer of foil, then strain the stock to get rid of the vegetables and spices. Return the stock to the pan.

4. Prepare the glass noodles according to the packet instructions and divide between four bowls. Cook the mushrooms and pak choi in the beef stock for 3 minutes or until tender, while you slice the beef.

5. Divide the beef, pak choi and mushrooms between the bowls and ladle some stock over each. Garnish with chillies and serve immediately.

Chicken and shiitake conge

SERVES: 6 | PREP TIME: 30 MINUTES | COOKING TIME: 1 HOUR

INGREDIENTS

30 g / 1 oz / ½ cup dried shiitake mushrooms

700 g / 1 lb 9 oz / 5 cups skinless chicken thighs,
on the bone

4 spring onions (scallions), chopped,
green and white parts separated

5 cm (2 in) fresh root ginger, half thickly sliced,
half finely julienned

200 g / 7 oz / 1 cup long-grain rice

1 litre / 17 ½ fl. oz / 4 cups chicken stock

100 g / 3 ½ oz / ½ cup canned bamboo shoots,
finely julienned

METHOD

1. Soak the shiitakes in boiling water for 20 minute
    then drain and thinly slice.

2. Put the shiitakes in a large saucepan with the
    chicken, spring onion whites, sliced ginger and
    rice. Cover with the chicken stock and 1.5 litres o
    water, then stir in 2 teaspoons of salt.

3. Bring the mixture to the boil, then reduce the hea
    and simmer for 1 hour or until the rice has broke
    down into a thick porridge, stirring occasionally.

4. Transfer the chicken to a chopping board, remo
    the bones and slice it thickly. Stir the chicken ba
    into the pot, then taste and adjust the seasonin
    with salt and white pepper. Ladle the congee int
    six bowls and top with julienned ginger, bambo
    shoots and spring onion greens.

Steamed siu mai

SERVES: 2 | PREP TIME: 30 MINUTES | COOKING TIME: 10 MINUTES

INGREDIENTS

300 g / 10 ½ oz chicken mince

150 g / 5 ¼ oz prawns, chopped

1 tbsp ginger, chopped

1 clove of garlic, minced

2 spring onions (scallions), chopped

½ tsp sesame oil

½ white pepper

1 tsp soy sauce

pinch of chilli (chili) flakes

300 g / 10 ½ oz wonton wrappers

METHOD

1. Combine all of the ingredients, except the wrappers, in a bowl and mix thoroughly to combine. Set aside in the refrigerator to chill for 20 minutes.

2. Lay the wrappers on a clean dry surface. Spoon the mixture into the centre of a wrapper and gather up the edges, leaving the top exposed. Trim off any excess wrapper.

3. Repeat the above step until all the mixture has been used.

4. Place a bamboo steamer over a pan of not quite boiling water. Steam the siu mai in the steamer for around 5 minutes.

5. Serve immediately with soy or a chilli dipping sauce.

Fried chicken wontons

SERVES: 2-4 | PREP TIME: 25 MINUTES | COOKING TIME: 10 MINUTES

INGREDIENTS

vegetable oil, for deep frying

300 g / 10 ½ oz chicken mince

1 clove of garlic, minced

2 spring onions (scallions), sliced

1 tsp light soy sauce

1 tsp oyster sauce

1 tbsp coriander (cilantro), chopped

a pinch of chilli (chili) flakes

1 egg beaten

20 wonton wrappers

METHOD

1. Heat the oil in a deep fat fryer to 180°C / 350F. Alternatively, heat enough oil in a wok to shallow fry.

2. Combine the chicken, garlic, spring onions, soy sauce, oyster sauce, coriander and chilli flakes in a bowl. Add a splash of water to the beaten egg and place into a bowl.

3. To make the wontons, place a wrapper into your hand and place a teaspoon of the chicken mixture into the centre of the wrapper. Using your fingertip, place egg wash about the edges of the wrapper and fold into a triangle, ensuring there are no air pockets, and seal. Carefully place the wontons into the oil and cook for 1-2 minutes each until golden brown. Remove with a slotted spoon and drain onto kitchen paper.

Lion's head meatballs

ERVES: 4 | PREP TIME: 45 MINUTES | COOKING TIME: 10-14 MINUTES

INGREDIENTS

450 g / 1 lb minced pork

/ 5 ½ oz / 1 cup water chestnuts, finely chopped

1 tsp fresh root ginger, finely grated

4 spring onions (scallions), chopped

50 ml / 1 ¾ fl. oz / ¼ cup Shaoxing rice wine

2 tbsp light soy sauce / 1 tbsp dark soy sauce

1 tbsp sesame oil

1 tbsp caster (superfine) sugar

3 medium eggs, beaten

1 tbsp cornflour (cornstarch)

100 g / 3 ½ oz / 1 cup panko breadcrumbs

2 tbsp vegetable oil

1 tbsp sesame seeds

METHOD

1. Put the pork in a large mixing bowl and beat in 60 ml of cold water. Add the water chestnuts, ginger and spring onion whites.

2. Whisk the rice wine with the soy sauces, sesame oil, sugar and eggs, then slowly mix into the pork mixture. Mix the cornflour and breadcrumbs, then work into the pork.

3. Shape the mixture into 16 meatballs, then cover and chill in the fridge for 30 minutes. Heat the vegetable oil in a large frying pan and sear the meatballs until browned. Transfer the meatballs to a steamer and steam for 15 minutes.

4. Skewer each meatball onto a wooden cocktail fork and transfer to a serving plate. Drizzle over the cooking juices and sprinkle with sesame seeds and spring onion greens.

Breakfast bao buns

SERVES: 2-4 | PREP TIME: 2 HOURS | COOKING TIME: 20 MINUTES

INGREDIENTS

1 tsp fast acting yeast

250 g / 9 oz / 1 ⅔ cups strong white bread flour

25 g / 1 oz caster (superfine) sugar

1 tsp salt

6 rashers streaky bacon

4 eggs

2 carrots, shredded

½ cucumber, sliced

2 red chillies (chili), sliced

METHOD

1. Add the yeast to a jug of 125ml warm water, cover and leave for 2-3 minutes to activate.

2. Combine the flour, sugar and salt in a bowl. Pour in the water and mix to combine, adding a little more water if too dry.

3. Turn out onto a floured surface and knead for 10 minutes. Cover with a damp tea towel and leave in a warm place to prove for 1 hour or until doubled in size.

4. Cut sheets of greaseproof paper into squares roughly 20 cm / 8 inch square.

5. Knock back the dough and divide into six equal sized balls. Roll out into oval shapes to fit the squares of greaseproof paper. Place onto a square of paper before placing another on top, fold to sandwich the paper. Place onto a tray and cover with cling film, then leave to prove again for 30 minutes.

6. Place a steamer on the heat and steam the buns for 8-10 minutes until puffy and cooked through. Remove from the steamer and remove the paper.

7. Cook the bacon in a frying pan until crispy, then fry the eggs in the same pan.

8. Fill the buns with the cooked bacon and eggs, followed by the carrot, cucumber and chilli

Beef and rice noodle soup

SERVES: 4 | PREP TIME: 30 MINUTES | COOKING TIME: 2 HOURS

INGREDIENTS

4 large shallots, unpeeled

8 cloves

25 g / 1 oz fresh root ginger, in one piece

2 parsnips, cut into large chunks

900 g / 2 lb meaty beef bones (e.g. oxtail)

1 tbsp white peppercorns

2 star anise

1 tbsp caster (superfine) sugar

50 ml / 1 ¾ fl. oz / ¼ cup fish sauce

300 g / 10 ½ oz flat rice noodles

1 small fillet steak, very thinly sliced

1 handful bean sprouts

2 chillies (chilies), sliced

½ red onion, thinly sliced

handful fresh coriander (cilantro) leaves

METHOD

1. Stud the shallots with cloves, then toast them under a hot grill with the ginger and parsnips until brown all over.

2. Transfer the vegetables to a large saucepan and add the bones, peppercorns, star anise, sugar and fish sauce. Pour over 1.5 litres of water.

3. Bring to the boil, then cover and simmer gently for 2 hours. Strain the broth to get rid of the bones and vegetables, then return it to the pan and bring to a simmer.

4. Prepare the noodles according to the packet instructions and divide between four bowls. Top with the raw steak, bean sprouts, chillies and onion, then ladle over the hot broth. Garnish with coriander leaves and serve immediately.

Roast pork belly noodles

SERVES: 6 | PREP TIME: 20 MINUTES + OVERNIGHT
COOKING TIME: 1 HOUR, 45 MINUTES

INGREDIENTS

1.5 kg / 3 lb 12 ½ oz boneless pork belly,
skin pricked all over

50 ml / 1 ¾ fl. oz / ¼ cup light soy sauce

2 tsp Chinese five spice

400 g / 14 oz thin egg noodles

1 tbsp vegetable oil

1 tbsp fresh root ginger, sliced

2 cloves of garlic, sliced

1.2 litres / 2 pints / 4 ¾ cups pork or chicken stock

1 orange pepper, quartered, deseeded and sliced

2 pak choi, leaves separated

6 poached eggs, to serve

2 large salad onions, whites sliced into rings,
greens chopped

soy sauce with chilli, for dipping

METHOD

1. Put the pork belly on a trivet in the sink, skin side up, and pour over a kettle of boiling water.

2. Dry thoroughly with kitchen paper, then rub 1 teaspoon of salt into the skin.

3. Mix the soy sauce and five spice in a wide bowl, then add the pork, flesh side down. Marinate, uncovered, in the fridge overnight.

4. Preheat the oven to its highest temperature. Transfer the pork to a roasting tin and dry the skin thoroughly. Roast for 30 minutes.

5. Reduce the temperature to 160°C (140°C fan) / 325F / gas 3 and roast for 1 hour.

6. Cook the noodles in boiling water according to the packet instructions, then drain well and divide between six warm bowls.

7. Heat the oil in a large wok and fry the ginger and garlic for 2 minutes. Add the stock and bring to the boil. Add the pepper and pak choi and simmer for 2 minutes.

8. Remove the crackling from the pork and break into chunks. Cut the pork into bite-sized pieces. Divide the pak choi, peppers and poached eggs between the bowls and ladle over the broth. Top with pork, crackling and salad onions and serve with soy sauce for dipping.

Beef spring rolls

SERVES: 4-6 | PREP TIME: 20 MINUTES | COOKING TIME: 30 MINUTES

INGREDIENTS

1 tbsp vegetable oil

500 g / 1 lb 1 oz beef mince

½ onion, diced

1 tsp Chinese five spice

2 cloves of garlic, minced

2 carrots, grated

15 g / ½ oz ginger, grated

1 tbsp soy sauce

1 tbsp rice wine

1 tsp Sichuan pepper, ground

1 tsp chilli (chili) flakes

300 g / 10 ½ oz spring roll wrappers

oil for frying

METHOD

1. Heat the oil in a frying pan over a moderate heat. Once hot add the beef and onion and cook for 3-4 minutes until browned and any liquid from the meat has started to evaporate.

2. Add the five spice, garlic, carrots and ginger and continue to cook for a further 2-3 minutes until fragrant.

3. Stir through the soy, wine, pepper and chilli flakes and taste to check the flavours are balanced. Remove from the heat and set aside to cool.

4. Once cooled, place a spring roll wrapper on a clean dry surface. Place a small cigar shaped piece of filling at one end of the wrapper. Roll once to contain the meat and then fold over the edges before rolling completely. Seal the end with a little water. Repeat until all the filling has been used.

5. Preheat the oil in a fryer to 180°C / 350F or alternatively fill a wok with enough oil to fry over a medium heat.

6. Cook the rolls in batches in the hot oil until crisp and golden, approximately 2-3 minutes, before draining on kitchen paper.

7. Serve with a dipping sauce and vegetables as desired.

Cook's Corner

Everyday Chinese
Fish dishes

Baked scallop wontons

MAKES: 12 | PREP TIME: 30 MINUTES | COOKING TIME: 15 MINUTES

INGREDIENTS

150 g / 5 ½ oz / 1 cup raw prawns (shrimp), finely chopped

1 tsp fresh root ginger, finely grated

1 spring onion (scallion), very finely chopped

1 tsp Shaoxing rice wine

1 tsp caster (superfine) sugar

1 tsp cornflour (cornstarch)

12 fresh scallops, shelled and cleaned

24 wonton wrappers

1 egg white, beaten

2 tbsp vegetable oil

chives, to garnish

METHOD

1. Preheat the oven to 200°C (180°C fan) / 400F / gas 6.

2. Mix the chopped prawns with the ginger, spring onion, rice wine, sugar and cornflour. Season with ½ a teaspoon of salt and some freshly ground white pepper.

3. Divide the prawn mixture into twelve and shape each piece around a scallop.

4. Brush the wonton wrappers with egg white and wrap two around each scallop to completely enclose.

5. Brush the wontons with oil and space them out on an oiled baking tray.

6. Bake the wontons for 15 minutes or until pale brown and crisp. The scallops should only just be cooked in the centre.

7. Serve immediately, garnished with chives.

Prawn and vegetable fried rice

SERVES: 4 | PREP TIME: 30 MINUTES | COOKING TIME: 15 MINUTES

INGREDIENTS

200 g / 7 oz raw king prawns,
peeled with tails left intact

2 tbsp yellow bean sauce

30 g dried wood ear fungus

2 tbsp vegetable oil

4 spring onions (scallions), chopped,
white and green parts separated

2 cloves of garlic, crushed

1 tbsp root ginger, finely chopped

½ red pepper, deseeded, quartered and sliced

½ yellow pepper, deseeded, quartered and sliced

½ carrot, julienned

200 g / 7 oz / 1 cup canned bamboo shoots, sliced

100 g / 3 ½ oz / ⅔ cup peas, defrosted if frozen

75 g / 2 ½ oz / ⅔ cup bean sprouts

500 g / 17 ½ oz / 3 cups long-grain rice,
cooked and cooled

2 tbsp light soy sauce

2 tsp sesame oil

1 small bunch Chinese chives, cut into short lengths

METHOD

1. Mix the prawns with the yellow bean sauce and leave to marinate for 30 minutes. Meanwhile, soak the dried fungus in cold water.

2. Heat the vegetable oil in a large wok and fry the spring onion whites, garlic and ginger for 2 minutes. Add the prawns and stir-fry until opaque.

3. Add the vegetables and drained fungus and fry for 4 minutes.

4. Add the rice and stir-fry until piping hot – this should take about 4 minutes.

5. Season the rice with soy sauce, sesame oil and black pepper, then serve immediately, garnished with spring onion greens.

Tempura fish

SERVES: 2 | PREP TIME: 15 MINUTES | COOKING TIME: 10 MINUTES

INGREDIENTS

00 g / 3 ½ oz / ⅔ cup plain (all-purpose) flour,
plus extra for dusting

pinch of salt

1 egg, beaten

1 tbsp olive oil

150 ml / 5 ¼ fl. oz / ⅔ cup sparkling water

handful of coriander (cilantro), chopped

1 tsp chilli (chili) flakes

600 g / 1 lb 5 oz monkfish, cubed

2 tbsp paprika

oil for frying

100 g / 3 ½ oz noodles, cooked

1 carrot, shredded

1 tbsp sesame oil

1 tbsp soy sauce

25 g / 1 oz radish, thinly sliced

METHOD

Mix the flour and salt in a large mixing
bowl. Make a well in the centre and add the
egg, oil and sparkling water. Whisk to form a
smooth batter, then stir through half the
coriander and chilli.

1. Heat the oil in a deep fat fryer to 180°C / 350F.

2. Coat the fish with the paprika and a dusting
    of flour. Dip the fish into the batter and
    carefully place into the hot oil. Fry in
    batches for 4-5 minutes until golden, taking
    care not to overfill the fryer.

3. Place onto kitchen paper to drain off any
    excess oil before serving.

4. Combine the noodles and carrots and toss
    with the oil and soy sauce to coat.

5. Serve the battered fish with the noodles
    and garnish with the radish and
    remaining coriander.

Summer rolls

SERVES: 6 | PREP TIME: 30 MINUTES

INGREDIENTS

75 g / 2 ½ oz vermicelli rice noodles

6 rice paper wrappers

18 cooked king prawns, peeled

6 soft lettuce leaves

¼ cucumber, julienned

½ carrot, coarsely grated

soy sauce, for dipping

METHOD

1. Put the noodles in a bowl and pour over enough boiling water to cover by 5 cm (2 in). Leave to soak for 4 minutes, then drain well.

2. Dip the first rice paper wrapper in a bowl of cold water, then lay it out on a clean chopping board. Arrange three prawns across the middle, then lay a lettuce leaf on top and add some noodles, cucumber and carrot.

3. Fold over the sides of the wrapper, then roll it up to enclose the filling.

4. Repeat with the rest of the ingredients to form six rolls, then serve immediately with soy sauce for dipping.

Salmon poke bowl

SERVES: 1 | PREP TIME: 40 MINUTES | COOKING TIME: 30 MINUTES

INGREDIENTS

1 salmon fillet, cubed

1 tbsp soy sauce

1 tbsp sesame oil

1 tsp rice vinegar

1 tbsp mixed sesame seeds

50 g / 1 ¾ oz / ¼ cup long-grain rice

¼ cucumber, sliced

100 g / 3 ½ oz pineapple chunks

50 g / 1 ¾ oz pickled seaweed

½ watermelon radish, sliced

METHOD

1. Combine the salmon with the soy, sesame, rice vinegar and sesame in a bowl. Toss to coat and leave in the refrigerator for 30 minutes to marinate.

2. Cook the rice as per the packet instructions, then drain well and set aside.

3. Place the rice into a bowl and top with the salmon, cucumber, pineapple, seaweed and radish.

4. Drizzle over any of the remaining marinade from the salmon.

Prawn noodle salad

SERVES: 4 | PREP TIME: 25 MINUTES | COOKING TIME: 10 MINUTES

INGREDIENTS

30 g / 1 oz / ½ cup dried wood ear fungus

400 g / 14 oz vermicelli rice noodles

150 g / 5 ½ oz / 1 cup sugar snap peas

½ red pepper, deseeded and chopped

½ yellow pepper, deseeded and chopped

½ carrot, peeled and julienned

½ spring onion, finely chopped

1 handful bean sprouts

75 g / 2 ½ oz / ½ cup frozen peas, defrosted

12 cooked king prawns

1 lime, juiced

1 tbsp soy sauce

1 tbsp caster (superfine) sugar

1 tbsp sesame oil

METHOD

1. Soak the fungus in cold water for 20 minutes then drain and thinly slice.

2. Meanwhile, cook the noodles according to the packet instructions, then drain and plunge into iced water. Drain well.

3. Blanch the sugar snap peas in boiling water for 3 minutes, then plunge into iced water and drain well.

4. Toss the noodles with the fungus, vegetables and prawns.

5. Mix the lime juice with the soy sauce, sugar and sesame oil, then toss the dressing with the salad. Refrigerate until you are ready to serve.

Barbecued red mullet

ERVES: 4 | PREP TIME: 1 HOUR 15 MINUTES | COOKING TIME: 6 MINUTES

INGREDIENTS

2 tbsp light soy sauce

2 lemons, 1 juiced, 1 halved and sliced

2 tbsp runny honey

50 ml / 1 ¾ fl. oz / ¼ cup Shaoxing rice wine

1 tsp sesame oil

8 red mullet, gutted and scaled

2 tbsp vegetable oil

METHOD

1. Whisk the soy sauce with the lemon juice, honey, rice wine and sesame oil. Pour the mixture over the fish, then marinate in the fridge for 1 hour.

2. Dry the mullet thoroughly with kitchen paper, then brush with oil and season liberally with salt and pepper. This will help to prevent them from sticking. Add a slice of lemon to the belly cavity of each one.

3. Make sure the metal barbecue grill is very hot before adding the fish. Cook over medium-hot coals for 3 minutes on each side or until the skin is brown and blistered and the flesh pulls easily away from the bones at the thickest part by the head.

123

Open crab dim sum

MAKES: 24 | PREP TIME: 30 MINUTES | COOKING TIME: 12 MINUTES

INGREDIENTS

100 g / 3 ½ oz / ⅔ cup white crab meat

75 g / 2 ½ oz / ½ cup raw prawns, chopped

½ carrot, peeled and grated

1 red chilli (chili), finely chopped

1 tsp fresh root ginger, finely grated

2 tsp light soy sauce

1 tsp caster (superfine) sugar

1 tsp sesame oil

1 tsp cornflour (cornstarch)

100 g / 3 ½ oz / ⅔ cup brown crab meat

24 round wonton wrappers

chives, to garnish

METHOD

1. Preheat the oven to 220°C (200°C fan) / 425F / gas 7 and oil a 24-hole mini muffin tin that will fit inside a roasting tin.

2. Mix the white crab meat and prawns with the carrot, chilli, ginger, soy sauce, sugar, sesame oil and cornflour.

3. Add a spoonful of brown crab meat to the centre of each wonton wrapper and spread it into a circle. Top each one with a spoonful of filling, then transfer to the muffin tin, allowing the edges to pleat in.

4. Add 2.5 cm (1 in) of boiling water to the roasting tin and carefully lower in the muffin tin. Cover the roasting tin tightly with foil, then transfer to the oven to steam for 12 minutes.

Chilli prawn stir-fry

SERVES: 4 | PREP TIME: 5 MINUTES | COOKING TIME: 20 MINUTES

INGREDIENTS

400 g / 14 oz thin egg noodles

2 tbsp sunflower oil

3 cloves of garlic, finely chopped

1 tbsp fresh root ginger, finely chopped

2 red chillies (chilies), finely chopped

½ tsp dried red chilli (chili) flakes

½ red, yellow and green peppers, quartered, deseeded and thinly sliced

00 g / 10 ½ oz / 2 cups raw king prawns, peeled

50 ml / 1 ¾ fl. oz / ¼ cup Shaoxing rice wine

2 tbsp soy sauce

1 tsp sesame oil

2 tbsp peanuts, finely chopped

METHOD

1. Cook the noodles according to the packet instructions, then drain and plunge into iced water. Drain well.

2. Heat the oil in a large wok and fry the garlic, ginger, chillies and chilli flakes for 3 minutes.

3. Add the peppers and prawns and stir-fry for 5 minutes or until the prawns have turned opaque.

4. Add the rice wine, soy and sesame oil and heat until it starts to simmer, then stir in the noodles. Stir-fry for 2 more minutes, then serve straight away, sprinkled with peanuts.

125

Steamed eggs with prawns

SERVES: 1 | PREP TIME: 5 MINUTES | COOKING TIME: 10 MINUTES

INGREDIENTS

2 large eggs

100 ml / 3 ½ fl. oz / ½ cup fish stock

½ tsp fresh root ginger, finely grated

3 raw king prawns, butterflied

coriander (cilantro) leaves, to garnish

METHOD

1. Whisk the eggs with the fish stock and a pinch of salt in a small heatproof bowl.

2. Transfer the bowl to a steamer and steam for 7 minutes.

3. Sprinkle with ginger and add the prawns, then cover and steam again for 3 minutes or until the egg has set.

4. Serve immediately.

Stuffed abalone

SERVES: 12 | PREP TIME: 5 MINUTES | COOKING TIME: 10 MINUTES

INGREDIENTS

2 tbsp vegetable oil

2 spring onions (scallions), finely chopped,
white and green parts separated

1 clove of garlic, crushed

1 tsp root ginger, finely grated

12 small live abalone or oysters,
shucked and half-shells reserved

200 g / 7 oz / 1 ¼ cups jasmine rice,
cooked and cooled

2 tbsp oyster sauce

1 tsp sesame oil

large mild red chillies (chilies), finely chopped

METHOD

1. Heat the vegetable oil in a large wok and fry
    the spring onion whites, garlic and ginger for
    2 minutes.

2. Add the abalone and stir-fry for 2 minutes or
    until opaque. Remove the abalone from the
    pan and roughly chop.

3. Add the rice to the wok and stir-fry until piping
    hot – this should take about 4 minutes.

4. Season the rice with oyster sauce and sesame oil,
    then return the abalone and stir-fry for 1 minute.

5. Spoon the rice into the reserved shells and
    sprinkle with chilli and spring onion greens.

127

Deep fried soft shell crabs

SERVES: 4 | PREP TIME: 20 MINUTES | COOKING TIME: 5 MINUTES

INGREDIENTS

2 tbsp vegetable oil, plus extra for deep frying

75 g / 2 ½ oz / ½ cup plain (all-purpose) flour

1 large egg, separated

150 ml / 5 ½ fl. oz / ⅔ cup sparkling water

8 soft shell crabs, cleaned and trimmed

8 kaffir lime leaves

1 large red chilli (chili), deseeded and sliced

2 cloves of garlic, sliced

50 g / 1 ¾ oz / ⅔ cup fresh green peppercorns

METHOD

1. Heat the oil in a deep fat fryer, according to the manufacturer's instructions, to a temperature of 180°C (350F).

2. Put 60 g of flour in a bowl and make a well in the middle. Add the egg yolk and sparkling water, then whisk them together, gradually incorporating all the flour from round the outside. Whip the egg white until stiff, then fold it into the batter.

3. Toss the crabs with the rest of the flour and shake off any excess. Working in batches, dip the crabs in the batter, then deep-fry for 3 minutes or until crisp. Drain on plenty of kitchen paper.

4. Heat 2 tablespoons of oil in a large wok and fry the lime leaves, chilli, garlic and peppercorns for 1 minute or until fragrant. Season with salt and white pepper, then serve immediately with your favourite dipping sauce.

Prawn congee

SERVES: 6 | PREP TIME: 5 MINUTES | COOKING TIME: 1 HOUR, 10 MINUTES

INGREDIENTS

200 g / 7 oz / 1 cup jasmine rice

2.3 litres / 4 pints / 8 cups fish stock

2 tbsp dried shrimps

300 g / 10 ½ oz / 2 cups raw king prawns,
peeled and deveined

75 ml / 2 ½ fl. oz / ⅓ cup vegetable oil

2 cloves of garlic, finely chopped

spring onions (scallions), whites finely chopped,
greens cut into 2 cm lengths

75 g / 2 ½ oz / 1 cup fresh white breadcrumbs

1 tbsp fresh root ginger, coarsely grated

1 small bunch fresh coriander (cilantro),
roughly chopped

METHOD

1. Put the rice and all but 300 ml of the stock in a saucepan with ½ a teaspoon of salt. Bring the mixture to the boil, then reduce the heat and simmer for 1 hour or until the rice has broken down into a thick porridge, stirring occasionally.

2. Meanwhile, soak the dried shrimps in hot water for 30 minutes, then drain and dry well.

3. When the rice is ready, bring the rest of the stock to the boil in a small saucepan. Gently poach the prawns until they turn opaque, then strain the stock into the congee pan and stir well. Taste and adjust the seasoning with salt and white pepper if necessary.

4. Heat the vegetable oil in a wok and fry the garlic, spring onion whites and rehydrated shrimps for 1 minute.

5. Add the breadcrumbs and stir-fry until golden and crisp.

6. Ladle the congee into six bowls and top with the prawns and breadcrumb mixture. Garnish with grated ginger, spring onion greens and fresh coriander.

Shrimps with spicy noodles

SERVES: 4 | PREP TIME: 10 MINUTES | COOKING TIME: 4 MINUTES

INGREDIENTS

300 ml / 10 ½ fl. oz / 1 ¼ cup vegetable oil

6 cloves of garlic, finely chopped

1 tbsp fresh root ginger, finely chopped

25 g tiny dried shrimps, rinsed and dried (optional)

50 g / 1 ¾ oz / ⅓ cup chilli (chili) flakes

1 ½ tbsp soy sauce

1 tbsp runny honey

300 g / 10 ½ oz / 4 blocks plain noodles

1 large tomato, sliced

2 pak choi, halved

2 salted duck eggs, halved

1 mild red chilli (chili), sliced

METHOD

1. To make the chilli paste, heat the oil in a wok and fry the garlic and ginger for 2 minutes or until fragrant, but not coloured. Add the dried shrimps and fry for 1 minute.

2. Stir in ½ a teaspoon of salt, then take the pan off the heat and leave to cool for 30 seconds. Stir in the chilli flakes, followed by the soy sauce and honey. Transfer to a serving bowl and leave to cool.

3. Place a block of noodles in each of four bowls. Smear the top of each block with a heaped teaspoon of the chilli paste and add a few slices of tomato, half a pak choi and half a salted duck egg to each one. Garnish with sliced chilli.

4. Cover the noodles with boiling water and leave to soften for 4 minutes, or according to the packet instructions, before serving.

Spicy prawn skewers

SERVES: 4 | PREP TIME: 10 MINUTES | COOKING TIME: 4 MINUTES

INGREDIENTS

1 lime, juiced, plus a few wedges to garnish

1 tbsp sriracha chilli sauce

1 clove of garlic, crushed

1 tsp fresh root ginger, finely grated

1 tsp caster (superfine) sugar

1 tbsp light soy sauce

12 large raw king prawns, peeled with tails left intact

a few sprigs fresh coriander (cilantro), finely chopped, to garnish

METHOD

1. Mix the lime juice with the sriracha, garlic, ginger, sugar and soy sauce. Add the prawn and stir well to coat, then cover and marinat in the fridge for 1 hour.

2. Meanwhile, soak four wooden skewers in cold water for 20 minutes.

3. Thread three prawns onto each skewer, then cook under a hot grill for 2 minutes on each side or until they turn pink.

4. Serve immediately, garnished with coriander and lime wedges.

Salt and pepper whitebait

SERVES: 6 | PREP TIME: 10 MINUTES | COOKING TIME: 5 MINUTES

INGREDIENTS

sunflower oil, for deep frying

75 g / 2 ½ oz / ½ cup plain (all-purpose) flour

75 g / 2 ½ oz / ½ cup potato starch

1 tsp chilli (chili) powder

1 tsp ground Szechwan peppercorns

1 tsp ground black peppercorns

450 g / 1 lb / 3 cups fresh whitebait

METHOD

1. Heat the oil in a deep fat fryer, according to the manufacturer's instructions, to a temperature of 180°C (350F).

2. Mix the flour with the potato starch, chilli powder, Szechwan and black pepper and 1 teaspoon of salt. Toss the whitebait with the flour mixture to coat and shake off any excess.

3. Deep-fry in batches for 5 minutes or until crisp.

4. Transfer the whitebait to a kitchen paper lined bowl to remove any excess oil, then serve immediately.

Eel with honey pepper sauce

SERVES: 4 | PREP TIME: 5 MINUTES | COOKING TIME: 5 MINUTES

INGREDIENTS

200 ml / 7 fl. oz / ¾ cup runny honey

75 ml / 2 ½ fl. oz / ⅓ cup dark soy sauce

75 ml / 2 ½ fl. oz / ⅓ cup pineapple juice

2 tbsp rice wine vinegar

1 tsp freshly ground black pepper

1 clove of garlic, crushed

1 lemon, juiced

1 large eel, skinned, filleted and halved

1 tbsp sesame seeds

steamed rice, to serve

METHOD

1. Put the honey, soy, pineapple juice, vinegar, black pepper, garlic and lemon juice in a small saucepan. Stir over a low heat until it starts to simmer, then cook gently for 5 minutes or until syrupy.

2. Meanwhile, cook the eel fillets under a hot grill for 2 minutes on each side or until just cooked in the centre. Transfer to a chopping board and slice on the diagonal.

3. Serve the eel on a bed of rice. Spoon over the sauce and sprinkle with sesame seeds.

136

Tomato and garlic king prawns

SERVES: 4 | PREP TIME: 15 MINUTES | COOKING TIME: 2 MINUTES

INGREDIENTS

1 tbsp vegetable oil

2 cloves of garlic, sliced

3 medium tomatoes, diced

75 ml / 2 ½ fl. oz / ⅓ cup Shaoxing rice wine

1 tbsp light soy sauce

vegetable oil, for deep frying

75 g / 2 ½ oz / ½ cup cornflour (cornstarch)

300 g / 10 ½ oz / 2 cups raw king prawns,
peeled with tails left intact

thyme and rosemary, to garnish

METHOD

1. Heat 1 tablespoon of oil in a wok and fry the
   garlic for 1 minute. Add the tomatoes and
   rice wine and simmer for 2 minutes. Season
   to taste with soy sauce and set aside.

2. Heat the oil in a deep fat fryer, according to
   the manufacturer's instructions, to a
   temperature of 190°C (375F).

3. Toss the prawns with the cornflour and
   shake off any excess. Deep-fry in batches for
   2 minutes or until crisp.

4. Drain on plenty of kitchen paper, then toss
   with the sauce and serve immediately,
   garnished with thyme and rosemary.

137

Prawn laksa

SERVES: 2 | PREP TIME: 10 MINUTES | COOKING TIME: 20 MINUTES

INGREDIENTS

1 tsp vegetable oil

2 tbsp laksa paste

1 tsp Chinese five spice

1 tsp tamarind

225 g / 8 oz canned bamboo shoots, drained

200 g / 7 oz bean sprouts

¼ white cabbage, shredded

400 ml / 13 ½ fl. oz / 1 ⅔ cups coconut milk

100 g / 3 ½ oz egg noodles.

120 g / 4 ¼ oz raw king prawns, shelled and deveined

1 lime, juiced

METHOD

1. Heat the oil in a wok or frying pan. Add the laksa paste, five spice and tamarind and fry for 1-2 minutes until fragrant.

2. Add the bamboo shoots, bean sprouts and cabbage and fry for 2-3 minutes until softened and coated in the paste.

3. Pour in the coconut milk, heat until boiling before turning down to a simmer. Allow to simmer and thicken for 10 minutes. In the meantime cook the noodles as per the packet instructions, drain and set aside.

4. Add the prawns to the soup and cook for 5 minutes until pink and firm. Squeeze the lime juice into the soup and season to taste.

5. Divide the noodles between serving bowls and top with the soup.

138

Salmon sushi rolls

SERVES: 2 | PREP TIME: 20 MINUTES

INGREDIENTS

150 g / 5 ¼ oz / ¾ cup sushi rice

1 tbsp rice vinegar

1 tsp caster (superfine) sugar

2 nori sheets

300 g / 10 ½ oz smoked salmon

100 g / 3 ½ oz cream cheese

1 avocado, peeled and sliced

100 g / 3 ½ oz keta salmon roe

2 tbsp soy sauce

1 tbsp black sesame seeds

METHOD

1. Cook the rice as per the packet instructions. Once cooked, set aside to cool before mixing through the vinegar and sugar.

2. Place a nori sheet onto a sushi mat that has been covered with cling film to prevent sticking. Coat with a handful of the cooled rice. Carefully turn over so that the nori sheet is facing you.

3. Top the nori sheet with the salmon, cream cheese, avocado and salmon roe, taking care not to overfill. Gently roll using the sushi mat to enclose the filling. Repeat until all the rice and filling has been used.

4. Drizzle the sushi rolls with the soy sauce and sprinkle over the sesame seeds before slicing and serving.

Prawn and spinach soup

SERVES: 4 | PREP TIME: 5 MINUTES | COOKING TIME: 15 MINUTES

INGREDIENTS

2 tbsp vegetable oil

2 cloves of garlic, finely chopped

2 tsp fresh root ginger, finely chopped

4 spring onions (scallions), chopped

2 tbsp Shaoxing rice wine

1 tsp caster (superfine) sugar

1 litre / 1 pint 14 fl. oz / 4 cups fish stock

100 g / 3 ½ oz / 3 cups spinach, washed

200 g / 7 oz / 1 ⅓ cups sugar snap peas

12 large king prawns, heads removed

1 tbsp dark soy sauce

1 handful fresh coriander (cilantro) leaves

METHOD

1. Heat the oil in a large wok and fry the garlic, ginger and spring onions for 2 minutes. Add the rice wine and sugar and stir-fry for 1 minute.

2. Add the fish stock and bring to the boil, then add the spinach. Cook for 1 minute, then blend until smooth in a liquidizer.

3. Return the soup to the wok and add the sugar snaps and prawns.

4. Simmer for 5 minutes, then season to taste with soy sauce.

5. Garnish with coriander and serve immediately.

Steamed prawn wontons

MAKES: 24 | PREP TIME: 30 MINUTES | COOKING TIME: 8 MINUTES

INGREDIENTS

225 g / 8 oz raw prawns (shrimp), chopped

2 canned water chestnuts, finely chopped

1 tsp fresh root ginger, finely grated

1 tsp Shaoxing rice wine

1 tsp caster (superfine) sugar

1 tsp sesame oil

1 tsp cornflour (cornstarch)

24 wonton wrappers

1 egg white, beaten

¼ Chinese cabbage, cubed (optional)

METHOD

1. Mix the chopped prawns with the water chestnuts, ginger, rice wine, sugar, sesame oil and cornflour. Season with 1 teaspoon of salt and some freshly ground white pepper.

2. Add a teaspoon of the mixture to the centre of each wonton wrapper. Brush round the outside with egg white, then draw up the sides of each wrapper and squeeze just above the filling to make a sack shape.

3. Space out the wontons in oiled steamer baskets, adding some Chinese cabbage to each if you prefer.

4. Steam the wontons for 8 minutes, then serve immediately.

141

Cheong fun

SERVES: 36 | PREP TIME: 45 MINUTES | COOKING TIME: 10 MINUTES

INGREDIENTS

125 g / 4 ½ oz / ½ cup dried shrimps

250 g / 9 oz / 1 ⅔ cups white rice flour

75 g / 2 ½ oz / ½ cup tapioca flour

40 g / 1 ½ oz / ¼ cup cornflour (cornstarch)

50 ml / 1 ¾ fl. oz / ¼ cup vegetable oil,
plus extra for brushing

3 mild red chillies (chilies),
deseeded and thinly julienned

1 bunch chives, half cut into short lengths,
half chopped

chilli (chili) oil, for dipping

METHOD

1. Soak the shrimps in cold water for 1 hour,
then drain and dry thoroughly
with kitchen paper.

2. Mix the three flours together, then rub in
the oil. Gradually incorporate 900 ml of cold
water to make a batter.

3. Line a small rectangular baking tray that
will fit inside your steamer with a layer of
wet muslin and preheat the steamer to high.
Brush a large chopping board with oil.

4. Ladle enough batter into the tray to cover the
bottom, then sprinkle with some of the
prawns, chillies and short chive lengths.
Cover and steam for 3 minutes or until
set and opaque.

5. Use a silicone spatula to prise the cheong fun
away from the muslin, rolling it up as you go,
then transfer to the chopping board, brush
with oil and cut into short lengths.

6. Repeat until all of the batter has been used,
then sprinkle with chopped chives and serve
with chilli oil for dipping.

143

Squid with black bean sauce

SERVES: 4 | PREP TIME: 10 MINUTES | COOKING TIME: 5 MINUTES

INGREDIENTS

4 large squid tubes, cleaned

2 tbsp vegetable oil

2 cloves of garlic, finely chopped

1 tbsp root ginger, finely chopped

2 spring onions (scallions),
cut into short lengths

2 red chillies (chilies), sliced

2 tbsp fermented black beans, rinsed and mashed

2 tbsp Shaoxing rice wine

1 tbsp dark soy sauce

1 tbsp oyster sauce

½ tsp cornflour (cornstarch)

steamed rice, to serve

1 handful fresh coriander (cilantro), chopped

METHOD

1. Open out the squid tubes and score the inside at 3 mm intervals. Cut the squid into bite sized pieces and set aside.

2. Heat the vegetable oil in a large wok and fry the garlic and ginger for 1 minute. Add the spring onions, chillies and black beans and fry for 1 minute.

3. Add the rice wine, soy and oyster sauce and stir well. Slake the cornflour with 3 tablespoons of cold water, add it to the pan and stir until thickened.

4. Add the squid and stir-fry for 1 minute or until it curls up and turns opaque.

5. Serve immediately on a bed of rice, sprinkled with coriander.

Spicy seafood soup

SERVES: 4 | PREP TIME: 15 MINUTES | COOKING TIME: 8 MINUTES

INGREDIENTS

3 medium squid tubes

3 red chillies (chilies), sliced,
plus extra to garnish

2 cloves of garlic, chopped

1 tbsp vegetable oil

1 tbsp fresh root ginger, very thinly sliced

2 stalks lemongrass, bruised

3 spring onions (scallions), whites chopped,
greens cut into short lengths

1 litre / 1 pint 14 fl. oz / 4 cups fish stock

2 tbsp Shaoxing rice wine

2 tsp caster (superfine) sugar

1 tbsp light soy sauce

g / 7 oz / 1 cup canned straw mushrooms, drained

12 raw king prawns, peeled with tails
left intact

een lip mussels in the half-shell, defrosted if frozen

e juice and chopped fresh coriander (cilantro)

METHOD

1. Open out the squid tubes, then score the inside with a sharp knife in a diamond pattern. Cut into bite-sized chunks and set aside.

2. Pound the chillies in a pestle and mortar with a pinch of salt to a fine paste. Add the garlic and pound again.

3. Heat the oil in a large wok and stir-fry the paste with the ginger, lemongrass and spring onion whites for 2 minutes. Add the stock, rice wine, sugar and soy sauce and bring to the boil.

4. Add the mushrooms, prawns and mussels and poach until the prawns turn opaque. Add the squid and poach until the pieces curl up and turn opaque.

5. Season the soup to taste with lime juice and salt, then ladle into bowls and garnish with spring onion greens and chopped coriander.

Crispy king prawns

SERVES: 4 | PREP TIME: 15 MINUTES | COOKING TIME: 2 MINUTES

INGREDIENTS

vegetable oil, for deep frying

75 g / 2 ½ oz / ½ cup plain (all-purpose) flour

1 large egg, separated

150 ml / 5 ½ fl. oz / ⅔ cup sparkling water

300 g / 10 ½ oz / 2 cups raw king prawns, peeled with tails left intact

lemon slices and chopped parsley, to serve

METHOD

1. Heat the oil in a deep fat fryer, according to the manufacturer's instructions, to a temperature of 190°C (375F).

2. Put 60 g of flour in a bowl and make a well in the middle. Add the egg yolk and sparkling water, then whisk them together, gradually incorporating all the flour from round the outside. Whip the egg white until stiff, then fold it into the batter.

3. Toss the prawns with the rest of the flour and shake off any excess. Working in batches, dip the prawns in the batter, then deep-fry for 2 minutes or until crisp.

4. Drain on plenty of kitchen paper and serve immediately, garnished with lemon and parsley.

Low fat prawn toasts

SERVES: 4 | PREP TIME: 5 MINUTES | COOKING TIME: 4 MINUTES

INGREDIENTS

g / 3 ½ oz / ⅔ cup cooked prawns (shrimp), peeled

1 clove of garlic, squashed

2 slices fresh root ginger

1 lime, juiced

1 tsp caster (superfine) sugar

1 tbsp light soy sauce

4 slices baguette

2 tsp sesame oil

dill sprigs, to garnish

METHOD

1. Put the prawns in a bowl with the garlic, ginger, lime juice, sugar and soy sauce. Cover and leave to marinate in the fridge for 1 hour.

2. Toast the baguette slices on both sides under a hot grill, then brush them with sesame oil.

3. Drain the prawns and discard the garlic and ginger. Pile the prawns onto the toasts and garnish with dill.

Fried prawn wonton

SERVES: 2-4 | PREP TIME: 25 MINUTES | COOKING TIME: 10 MINUTES

INGREDIENTS

vegetable oil, for deep frying

300 g / 10 ½ oz / 4 cups raw king prawns, shelled and chopped

1 l / 35 fl. oz / 4 cups lemon, juiced

1 clove of garlic, minced

2 spring onions (scallions), sliced

1 tsp light soy sauce

1 tsp oyster sauce

1 tbsp coriander (cilantro), chopped

pinch of chilli (chili) flakes

1 egg beaten

20 wonton wrappers

METHOD

1. Heat the oil in a deep fat fryer to 180°C / 350F. Alternatively heat enough oil in a wok to shallow fry.

2. Combine the prawns, lemon, garlic, spring onions, soy sauce, oyster sauce, coriander and chilli flakes in a bowl. Add a splash of water to the beaten egg and place in a bowl.

3. To make the wontons, place a wrapper into your hand and place a teaspoon of the prawn mixture into the centre of the wrapper. Using your fingertip, place egg wash about the edges of the wrapper and fold into a triangle, ensuring there are no air pockets, and seal. Carefully place into the oil and cook for 1-2 minutes each until golden brown. Remove with a slotted spoon and drain onto kitchen paper.

Crab and sweetcorn soup

SERVES: 4 | PREP TIME: 15 MINUTES | COOKING TIME: 8 MINUTES

INGREDIENTS

00 g / 14 oz / 2 cups canned sweetcorn, drained

tre / 1 pint 14 fl. oz / 4 cups chicken or vegetable stock

2 tbsp vegetable oil

4 spring onions (scallions), finely chopped, white parts only

2 tsp fresh root ginger, finely chopped

2 red chillies (chilies), deseeded and chopped

2 tbsp Shaoxing rice wine

1 tsp cornflour (cornstarch)

200 g / 7 oz / 1 ⅓ cups fresh white crab meat

1 large egg, beaten

1-2 tbsp light soy sauce

METHOD

1. Put 150 g of the sweetcorn in a liquidizer with 150 ml of the stock and blend until smooth. Set aside.

2. Heat the oil in a large wok and fry the spring onions, ginger and chillies for 2 minutes. Add the rice wine and cook until evaporated, then pour in the stock and sweetcorn purée.

3. Slake the cornflour with 1 tablespoon of cold water. When the soup starts to boil, pour in the cornflour mixture and stir until thickened.

4. Add the crab meat and sweetcorn and stir until the soup simmers. Pass the beaten egg through a sieve directly into the soup, stirring to make thin strands of egg. Add soy sauce and serve immediately.

Crispy noodles and seafood

SERVES: 1 | PREP TIME: 15 MINUTES | COOKING TIME: 5 MINUTES

INGREDIENTS

1 small squid tube, cleaned

100 g / 3 ½ oz / 1 cup thin egg noodles

vegetable oil, for deep frying

1 tbsp sunflower oil

2 dried red chillies (chilies)

3 raw king prawns, peeled

1 handful mangetout

3 pak choi leaves

1 tbsp light soy sauce

METHOD

1. Open out the squid tube and score the inside with a sharp knife in a fine diamond pattern. Cut it into five pieces and set aside.

2. Blanch the noodles in boiling water for 2 minutes, then drain well. Spread them out on a clean tea towel and dry thoroughly with kitchen paper.

3. Heat the vegetable oil in a deep fat fryer, according to the manufacturer's instructions, to a temperature of 180°C (350F). Deep fry the noodles for 1 minute or until golden and crisp. Drain well on plenty of kitchen paper and keep warm in a low oven.

4. Heat the sunflower oil in a wok and fry the chillies and prawns for 1 minute. Add the mangetout and cook for 1 minute, then add the squid and pak choi. As soon as the squid curls up and turns opaque, season with soy sauce and take the wok off the heat.

5. Serve the seafood and vegetables on top of the noodles immediately.

Crab, pork and noodle soup

SERVES: 6 | PREP TIME: 10 MINUTES | COOKING TIME: 10 MINUTES

INGREDIENTS

300 g / 10 ½ oz coarsely minced pork

200 g / 7 oz crab meat (50/50 white and brown)

1 tsp red curry paste

3 large eggs, beaten

450 g / 1 lb thin rice noodles

1 tbsp vegetable oil

3 spring onions (scallions), finely chopped, white and green parts separated

2 cloves of garlic, finely chopped

3 medium tomatoes, diced

1 tbsp fish sauce

1 tbsp tamarind paste

holy basil, to garnish

METHOD

1. Mix the pork in a bowl with the crab, curry paste, eggs and 1 teaspoon of salt. Set aside.

2. Cook the noodles according to the packet instructions or until al dente. Plunge into cold water, then drain well.

3. Heat the oil in a large wok and fry the spring onion whites and garlic for 1 minute. Add the tomatoes and fish sauce and stir-fry for 2 minutes. Pour in 1.5 litres of boiling water and stir in the tamarind and 1 teaspoon of salt.

4. Scoop spoonfuls of the pork mixture into the boiling liquid. When it rises to the surface, stir in the noodles and taste the soup for seasoning.

5. Divide the soup between six bowls and garnish with spring onion greens and holy basil.

Prawn and shiitake salad

SERVES: 4 | PREP TIME: 25 MINUTES | COOKING TIME: 10 MINUTES

INGREDIENTS

30 g / 1 oz / ½ cup dried shiitake mushrooms

400 g / 14 oz flat rice noodles

200 g / 7 oz / 1 ⅓ cups cooked prawns (shrimp), peeled

4 spring onions (scallions), sliced

1 red chilli (chili), sliced

1 green chilli (chili), sliced

4 sprigs mint

1 tbsp caster (superfine) sugar

1 lime, juiced, plus extra wedges to serve

1 tbsp fish sauce

METHOD

1. Soak the shiitakes in boiling water for 20 minutes, then drain and thinly slice.

2. Meanwhile, cook the noodles according to the packet instructions, then drain and plunge into iced water. Drain well.

3. Divide the noodles between four bowls and top with the prawns, spring onions, chillies and mint.

4. Stir the sugar into the lime juice and fish sauce until it dissolves, then drizzle it over the salads. Serve immediately, with extra wedges of lime on the side.

Singapore fried rice vermicelli

SERVES: 2 | PREP TIME: 30 MINUTES | COOKING TIME: 20 MINUTES

INGREDIENTS

2 eggs, beaten

1 tsp curry powder

2 tbsp sesame oil

180 g / 6 oz raw king prawns, shelled

1 birds eye chilli (chili), chopped

1 in piece of root ginger, grated

1 red pepper, thinly sliced

1 green pepper, thinly sliced

¼ white cabbage, shredded

50 g / 5 ¼ oz rice vermicelli, cooked and drained

200 ml / 7 fl. oz / ¾ cup chicken stock

1 tbsp sesame seeds

METHOD

1. Whisk the eggs with a pinch of curry powder. Heat 1 tbsp oil in a wok and cook the egg for 2-3 minutes until they resemble an omelette. Remove from the pan and chop.

Add the remaining oil to the pan and cook the prawns for 1 minute, then add the chilli, ginger, peppers, cabbage and remaining curry powder. Continue cooking for 2-3 minutes until fragrant, stirring constantly.

2. Add the noodles to the pan and add the chicken stock. Continue to stir-fry until most of the liquid has been absorbed and the noodles are tender. Mix through the egg.

3. Divide between two serving plates and scatter over the sesame seeds.

157

Seaweed-wrapped dumplings

MAKES: 18 | PREP TIME: 50 MINUTES | COOKING TIME: 10 MINUTES

INGREDIENTS

350 g / 12 ½ oz raw prawns (shrimp), finely chopped

175 g / 6 oz minced pork

2 spring onions (scallions), finely chopped

2 mild orange chillies (chilies),
deseeded and very finely chopped

1 tsp fresh root ginger, finely grated

1 egg white

1 tbsp Shaoxing rice wine

1 tbsp cornflour (cornstarch)

3 sheets nori seaweed

METHOD

1. Mix the prawns with the pork, spring onions, chillies, ginger, egg white, rice wine and cornflour. Season with 1 tsp salt and some freshly ground white pepper.

2. Lay the nori sheets out on a chopping board, overlapping the seams by 1 cm. Top with the prawn mixture, then roll it up into a tight sausage.

3. Chill the sausage for 30 minutes, then cut it into 2.5 cm (1 in) slices with a very sharp knife.

4. Steam the dumplings for 10 minutes or until opaque in the centre, then serve immediately.

Sunflower prawn toasts

SERVES: 6 | PREP TIME: 40 MINUTES | COOKING TIME: 30 MINUTES

INGREDIENTS

150 g / 5 ½ oz raw prawns (shrimp), peeled

1 clove of garlic, crushed

1 tsp fresh root ginger, finely grated

½ tsp chilli (chili) paste

1 tbsp white rice flour

1 egg yolk

1 tsp soy sauce

1 tsp sesame oil

6 slices white bread

sunflower oil, for deep frying

50 g / 1 ¾ oz / ⅓ cup sunflower seeds

spring onion (scallion) greens, to garnish

METHOD

1. Put the prawns in a food processor with the garlic, ginger, chilli paste, rice flour, egg yolk, soy and sesame oil. Blend to a paste.

2. Divide the paste between the slices of bread and spread into an even layer. Cut each slice into four triangles.

3. Heat the oil in a deep fat fryer, according to the manufacturer's instructions, to a temperature of 180°C (350F).

4. Dip the prawn layer in sunflower seeds to coat, then fry the toasts in batches for 3 minutes, turning them over halfway through. Drain on plenty of kitchen paper, then serve immediately, garnished with spring onion greens.

Prawn and bamboo wonton soup

SERVES: 4 | PREP TIME: 30 MINUTES | COOKING TIME: 4 MINUTES

INGREDIENTS

225 g / 8 oz raw prawns (shrimp), chopped

5 g / 2 ½ oz bamboo shoots, finely chopped

ing onions (scallions), whites finely chopped, greens sliced

1 tsp fresh root ginger, finely grated

1 tsp Shaoxing rice wine

1 tsp caster (superfine) sugar

1 tsp sesame oil

1 tsp cornflour (cornstarch)

24 wonton wrappers

1 egg white, beaten

1 litre / 17 ½ fl. oz / 4 cups clear fish stock

1 tbsp soy sauce

handful fresh coriander (cilantro) leaves

METHOD

1. Mix the chopped prawns with the bamboo shoots, spring onion whites, ginger, rice wine, sugar, sesame oil and cornflour. Season with 1 teaspoon of salt and some freshly ground white pepper.

2. Add a teaspoon of the mixture to the centre of each wonton wrapper. Brush round the outside with egg white, then draw up the sides of each wrapper and squeeze just above the filling to make a sack shape.

3. Bring the stock to a simmer in a large saucepan. Add the wontons and poach for 4 minutes.

4. Divide the soup and wontons between four bowls and garnish with spring onion greens and coriander leaves.

Octopus noodle salad

SERVES: 4 | PREP TIME: 15 MINUTES | COOKING TIME: 50 MINUTES

INGREDIENTS

50 ml / 1 ¾ fl. oz / ¼ cup dark soy sauce

5 cm / 2 in fresh root ginger, sliced

1 bulb garlic, halved horizontally

1 octopus, frozen for at least 2 weeks and defrosted

400 g / 14 oz glass noodles

1 carrot, julienned

1 yellow pepper, deseeded and julienned

1 leek, sliced

150 g / 5 ½ oz / 1 cup sugar snap peas

75 g / 2 ½ oz / ½ cup peas, defrosted if frozen

1 tbsp caster (superfine) sugar

1 lime, juiced, plus extra wedges to serve

1 tbsp fish sauce

1 tbsp chives, chopped

1 tbsp sesame seeds

METHOD

1. Bring a large saucepan of water to the boil and stir in the dark soy, ginger and garlic. Submerge the octopus and simmer for 50 minutes or until tender.

2. Meanwhile, cook the noodles according to the packet instructions, then drain and plunge into iced water. Drain well.

3. Blanch the vegetables in boiling salted water for 2 minutes, then drain and plunge into iced water. Drain well

4. Divide the noodles and vegetables between four bowls. Discard the eyes and beak of the octopus and slice the rest, then arrange on top.

5. Stir the sugar into the lime juice and fish sauce until it dissolves, then drizzle it over the salads. Serve sprinkled with chives and sesame seeds.

Cook's Corner

Everyday Chinese
Vegetables dishes

Vegetable egg rolls

SERVES: 2-4 | PREP TIME: 30 MINUTES | COOKING TIME: 30 MINUTES

INGREDIENTS

1 tbsp sesame oil

2 cloves of garlic, chopped

1 in piece of root ginger, grated

1 red chilli (chili), chopped

2 carrots, grated

1 red pepper, thinly sliced

100 g / 3 ½ oz bean sprouts

100 g / 3 ½ oz mushrooms, chopped

½ white cabbage, shredded

2 tbsp soy sauce

1 tsp cornflour (cornstarch)

150 g / 5 ¼ oz spring roll wrappers

1 egg, beaten

METHOD

1. Preheat the oven to 200°C (180°C fan) / 400F / gas 6 and lightly grease and line a baking tray.

2. Heat the oil in a wok or frying pan and add the garlic, ginger and chilli. Cook for 2-3 minutes until fragrant.

3. Add the carrots, pepper, bean sprouts, mushrooms and white cabbage. Stir-fry for 4-5 minutes until softened and reduced in size.

4. Whisk together the soy sauce and cornflour and add to the pan. Toss to coat the ingredients with the soy. Remove from the pan and set aside to cool.

5. Once the mixture is cool you can make the rolls. Lay a sheet of spring roll wrapping on a clean and dry work surface. Place some of the mixture to one end of a sheet leaving room to fold over the ends. Carefully fold and then roll the wrapper sealing with a little water.

6. Place onto the prepared baking tray and repeat until all the filling has been used.

7. Lightly brush with the beaten egg and bake in the oven for 20 minutes until golden and crispy, turning once during cooking as required.

Mushroom noodle soup

SERVES: 4 | PREP TIME: 20 MINUTES | COOKING TIME: 10 MINUTES

INGREDIENTS

8 dried shiitake mushrooms

300 g / 10 ½ oz vermicelli rice noodles

1 litre / 1 pint 14 fl. oz / 4 cups
vegetable stock

2 tbsp Shaoxing rice wine

1 tsp caster (superfine) sugar

175 g / 6 oz / 1 ½ cups butternut squash,
julienned with a mandolin

175 g / 6 oz / 2 cups shimeji mushrooms

¼ leek, thinly sliced

1 handful coriander (cilantro) leaves

chilli bean paste and soy sauce, to serve

METHOD

1. Cover the shiitake mushrooms in boiling water and leave to soak for 20 minutes.

2. Meanwhile, cook the noodles in boiling water according to the packet instructions or until al dente. Plunge into cold water, then drain well and divide between four bowls.

3. Heat the stock in a saucepan with the rice wine and sugar. Strain the shiitake soaking liquor through a fine sieve and add it to the pan.

4. When it starts to boil, add the squash and simmer gently for 4 minutes or until tender. Scoop it out and divide between the bowls.

5. Add the shimeji to the broth and simmer for 3 minutes. Scoop out and divide between the bowls. Warm through the shiitake in the broth, then add to the bowls and ladle over the stock.

6. Garnish with leek and coriander and serve with chilli bean paste and soy sauce for seasoning at the table.

Vegetable fried rice

SERVES: 4 | PREP TIME: 5 MINUTES | COOKING TIME: 10 MINUTES

INGREDIENTS

2 tbsp vegetable oil

1 small onion, thinly sliced

2 cloves of garlic, crushed

1 tbsp root ginger, finely chopped

2 tsp mixed peppercorns, lightly crushed

1 romano pepper, deseeded and thinly sliced

1 Chinese aubergine (eggplant),
quartered and sliced

2 courgettes (zucchinis), thinly sliced

500 g / 17 ½ oz / 3 cups long-grain rice,
cooked and cooled

2 tbsp light soy sauce

2 tsp sesame oil

2 tbsp pine nuts, toasted

1 tbsp fresh dill, chopped

2 tbsp fresh coriander (cilantro), chopped

METHOD

1. Heat the vegetable oil in a large wok and fry
   the onion, garlic, ginger and peppercorns
   for 2 minutes.

2. Add the vegetables and fry for 4 minutes.

3. Add the rice and stir-fry until piping hot –
   this should take about 4 minutes.

4. Season the rice with soy sauce and sesame
   oil, then divide between four plates and
   garnish with pine nuts, dill and coriander.

Fried stuffed buns

SERVES: 6-8 | PREP TIME: 2 HOURS | COOKING TIME: 8 MINUTES

INGREDIENTS

1 tsp fast acting yeast

250 g / 9 oz / 1 ⅔ cups strong white bread flour

25 g / 1 oz caster (superfine) sugar

1 tsp salt

75 g / 2 ½ oz red bean paste

2 tbsp vegetable oil

2 tbsp black sesame seeds

METHOD

1. Add the yeast to a jug of 125ml warm water, cover and leave for 2-3 minutes to activate.

2. Combine the flour, sugar and salt in a bowl. Pour in the water and mix to combine, adding a little more water if too dry.

3. Turn out onto a floured surface and knead for 10 minutes. Cover with a damp tea towel and leave in a warm place to prove for 1 hour or until doubled in size.

4. Knock back the dough and divide into two. Roll into a thick sausage shape before cutting into 4 equal portions.

5. Flatten each portion into a circular shape before filling with roughly 1 tbsp of the bean paste. Seal the dough around the filling and place onto a lined baked tray, with the folds facing down. Repeat until all the dough has been used. Cover with a wet cloth and leave for up to an hour to prove a second time.

6. Heat the oil in a large heavy bottomed pan with a lid over a medium heat. Fry the buns in batches, first on one side with the lid on for around 6-8 minutes and then the other side for the same time with the lid removed. Sprinkle over the sesame seeds.

Kimchi

SERVES: 2-4 | PREP TIME: 2 HOURS | FERMENTING TIME: 48 HOURS

INGREDIENTS

1 kg / 1 lb 3 oz napa cabbage

2 tbsp sea salt

25 g / 1 oz / ¼ cup glutinous rice flour

1 onion, diced

10 cloves of garlic

15 g / ½ oz ginger, peeled

50 ml / 1 ¾ fl. oz / ¼ cup fish sauce

50 g / 1 ¾ oz Korean chilli (chili) flakes

150 g / 5 ¼ oz radish, julienned

2 carrots, grated

4 spring onions (scallions), roughly chopped

METHOD

1. Slice the cabbage into quarters. Remove the tough ends, before rinsing in cold water. Place into a bowl and massage in the salt. Cover and leave for 1-2 hours. Rinse with cold water to remove any excess salt.

2. Mix the rice flour with 300 ml of water and heat for 3-4 minutes until thick and opaque.

3. Place the onion, garlic and ginger into a food processor and blend to a paste. Add to the rice flour with the fish sauce, chilli, radish, carrots and spring onions.

4. Mix the cabbage into the other ingredients, thoroughly coating the cabbage. Store at room temperature for 48 hours to ferment. It will develop a tangy taste once ready.

Egg chilli noodles

SERVES: 4 | PREP TIME: 10 MINUTES | COOKING TIME: 3 MINUTES

INGREDIENTS

400 g / 14 oz thin egg noodles

2 tbsp vegetable oil

2 cloves of garlic, crushed

1 tbsp fresh root ginger, finely grated

2 tbsp light soy sauce

spring onions (scallions), chopped, greens only

3 red chillies (chilies), sliced

METHOD

1. Cook the noodles in boiling water according to the packet instructions or until al dente, then drain well.

2. Heat the oil in a large wok and fry the garlic and ginger for 1 minute. Add the noodles and stir-fry for 2 minutes, then toss with the soy sauce.

3. Serve immediately, sprinkled with spring onion greens and chillies.

Spicy tofu rice

SERVES: 2 | PREP TIME: 30 MINUTES | COOKING TIME: 20 MINUTES

INGREDIENTS

350 g / 12 ¼ oz tofu

1 tbsp olive oil

1 onion, diced

2 cloves of garlic, chopped

2 tsp chilli (chili) flakes

1 tsp Sichuan pepper, crushed

2 tsp soy sauce

1 tsp sesame oil

1 tsp honey

2 peppers, sliced

500 g / 1lb 1 oz / 2 ¾ cups cooked rice

100 ml / 3 ½ fl. oz / ½ cup vegetable stock.

METHOD

1. Wash and pat dry the tofu before cutting into cubes. Heat the oil in a frying pan over medium high heat. Once hot, add the tofu and fry for 4-5 minutes turning regularly. Remove from the pan and set aside.

2. Turn the heat down a little and add the onion. Fry for 4-5 minutes until softened. Add the garlic and cook for a further minute.

3. Whisk together the chilli, pepper, soy, sesame oil and honey. Add to the pan and allow to bubble and thicken for a minute before returning the tofu to the pan.

4. Add the peppers and stir-fry for 4-5 minutes. Add the rice and mix through. Add the stock to loosen the rice and cook the ingredients together for 5 minutes until warmed through. Check the seasoning and serve.

Vegetarian wonton soup

SERVES: 4 | PREP TIME: 45 MINUTES | COOKING TIME: 5 MINUTES

INGREDIENTS

30 g / 1 oz / ½ cup dried wood ear fungus

½ head broccoli, finely chopped

g / 3 ½ oz / ½ cup silken tofu, cut into 5 mm dice

1 tsp fresh root ginger, finely grated

1 tsp Shaoxing rice wine

1 tsp caster (superfine) sugar

1 tsp sesame oil

24 wonton wrappers

1 egg white, beaten

litre / 17 ½ fl. oz / 4 cups clear vegetable stock

3 baby pak choi, leaves separated

1 tbsp soy sauce

METHOD

1. Soak the fungus in cold water for 20 minutes, then drain and finely chop.

2. Mix the fungus with the broccoli, tofu, ginger, rice wine, sugar and sesame oil. Season with 1 teaspoon of salt and some freshly ground white pepper.

3. Add a teaspoon of the mixture to the centre of each wonton wrapper. Brush round the outside with egg white, then draw up the sides of each wrapper and squeeze just above the filling to make a sack shape.

4. Bring the vegetable stock to a simmer, then add the wontons and cook for 2 minutes. Add the pak choi and cook for 2 minutes or until the wontons are tender. Taste and add soy sauce as necessary. Ladle into four bowls.

Egg drop soup

SERVES: 2-4 | PREP TIME: 10 MINUTES | COOKING TIME: 15 MINUTES

INGREDIENTS

1 tsp vegetable oil

1 carrot, diced

1 shallot, diced

1 clove of garlic, minced

½ tsp turmeric

50 g / 1 ¾ oz spring greens, chopped

1 l / 35 fl. oz / 4 cups chicken stock

1 tbsp cornflour (cornstarch)

4 eggs, beaten

1 tbsp sesame oil

1 tsp sesame seeds

METHOD

1. In a large saucepan heat the oil over a medium heat and sweat the carrot, shallot and garlic together for 4-5 minutes until softened.

2. Stir through the turmeric and greens before adding the chicken stock. Turn up the heat until boiling before turning back down to simmer for 8-10 minutes. Season to taste.

3. Combine the cornflour with some water to create a paste. Mix through the soup to thicken.

4. Place the eggs into a bowl and drizzle gently through a fork into the soup, stir to break up into smaller pieces as desired. Drizzle over the sesame oil and seeds before serving.

Choy sum with ginger

SERVES: 4 | PREP TIME: 5 MINUTES | COOKING TIME: 3 MINUTES

INGREDIENTS

3 tbsp vegetable oil

300 g / 10 ½ oz choy sum, trimmed

3 spring onions (scallions), finely julienned

1 tbsp fresh root ginger, finely julienned

1 tbsp sesame oil

2 tbsp light soy sauce

METHOD

1. Bring a large saucepan of water to the boil and add 1 teaspoon of salt and 1 tablespoon of the vegetable oil. Blanch the choy sum for 2 minutes, then drain well and arrange on a warm serving plate. Top the choy sum with the spring onions and ginger.

2. Heat the rest of the vegetable oil with the sesame oil over a high heat until smoking hot, then pour it over the ginger and spring onions.

3. Dilute the soy sauce with 2 tablespoons of boiling water, then pour it over the choy sum. Serve immediately.

Kimchi rice with egg

SERVES: 2 | PREP TIME: 5 MINUTES | COOKING TIME: 10 MINUTES

INGREDIENTS

200 g / 7 oz kimchi (see recipe in Vegetable Dishes)

1 tbsp red chilli (chili) paste

1 tsp soy sauce

2 tsp sesame oil

500 g / 1 lb 1 oz / 2 ¾ cups cooked short-grain rice

2 tbsp vegetable oil

2 eggs

2 spring onions (scallions), sliced

METHOD

1. Squeeze the kimchi over a bowl to collect the juice. Whisk this together with the chilli paste and soy.

2. Drizzle the sesame oil over the cooked rice and break up into smaller pieces. You need to have cold rice for this recipe to work best

3. Heat half the vegetable oil in a pan or wok over a medium high heat. Add the kimchi and fry for 3-4 minutes until fragrant and the kimchi has browned.

4. Add the rice and continue to fry, mixing the rice through the kimchi and reheating it thoroughly.

5. Pour the wet ingredients into the pan and toss to coat the rice thoroughly. Continue to cook, stirring regularly until hot through. Divide between two serving plates.

6. Add the remaining oil to the pan and fry the two eggs, place on top of the rice.

7. Scatter over the sliced spring onions before serving.

Tofu and mushroom soup

SERVES: 4 | PREP TIME: 15 MINUTES | COOKING TIME: 8 MINUTES

INGREDIENTS

2 red chillies (chilies), sliced

1 clove of garlic, chopped

1 tsp fresh root ginger, chopped

1 litre / 1 pint 14 fl. oz / 4 cups vegetable stock

1 stalk lemongrass, bruised

2 kaffir lime leaves

2 tbsp Shaoxing rice wine

2 tsp caster (superfine) sugar

1 tbsp fish sauce

1 lime, cut into 8 wedges

150 g / 5 ½ oz / 2 cups chestnut mushrooms, halved and sliced

3 medium tomatoes, cut into wedges

200 g / 7 oz / 1 ⅓ cups tofu, sliced

holy basil and coriander (cilantro), to garnish

METHOD

1. Pound three of the chillies in a pestle and mortar with a pinch of salt to a fine paste. Add the garlic and pound again, followed by the ginger.

2. Heat the stock in a large saucepan and dissolve the paste into it. Add the lemongrass, lime leaves, rice wine, sugar and fish sauce and simmer for 5 minutes.

3. Add the lime, mushrooms, tomatoes and tofu and simmer for 3 minutes.

4. Taste the soup and adjust the seasoning with salt, then ladle into bowls and serve, garnished with holy basil and coriander.

Mini vegetable spring rolls

MAKES: 24 | PREP TIME: 45 MINUTES | COOKING TIME: 3 MINUTES

INGREDIENTS

30 g / 1 oz / ½ cup dried shiitake mushrooms

1 tbsp vegetable oil, plus extra to deep fry

1 tsp fresh root ginger, finely chopped

2 clove of garlic, finely chopped

1 carrot, finely julienned

1 red pepper, deseeded and finely julienned

200 g / 7 oz / 1 cup canned bamboo shoots,
drained and finely julienned

2 spring onions (scallions), finely julienned

2 Chinese cabbage leaves, finely julienned

1 tsp Shaoxing rice wine

1 tsp caster (superfine) sugar

1 tsp cornflour (cornstarch)

1 tbsp light soy sauce

24 wonton wrappers

1 egg white, beaten

METHOD

1. Soak the mushrooms in cold water for
20 minutes, then drain and finely julienne.

2. Heat 1 tablespoon of vegetable oil in a wok
and fry the ginger and garlic for
1 minute. Add the carrot and peppers and
stir-fry for 2 minutes. Add the bamboo
shoots, spring onions, cabbage and shiitakes
and stir-fry for 1 minute.

3. Stir in the wine and sugar, then slake the
cornflour in the soy sauce and stir it in.
Stir-fry until there is no liquid left in the
bottom of the wok. Leave to cool, then chill
for 1 hour.

4. Brush the wonton wrappers with egg white,
then add a heaped teaspoonful of the
mixture to one side of each one. Fold the
wanton skin in half and press the edges
firmly to seal.

5. Heat the vegetable oil in a deep fat fryer,
according to the manufacturer's instructions,
to a temperature of 180°C (350F).

6. Fry the spring rolls in batches for 3 minutes
or until golden and crisp.

7. Drain on plenty of kitchen paper and
serve immediately.

Mushroom and egg noodles

SERVES: 2 | PREP TIME: 10 MINUTES | COOKING TIME: 15 MINUTES

INGREDIENTS

300 g / 10 ½ oz egg noodles

2 tbsp vegetable oil

3 eggs, beaten

1 tsp sesame oil

1 in piece of root ginger, chopped

2 cloves of garlic, chopped

1 red chilli (chili), diced

180 g / 6 oz chestnut mushrooms, chopped

50 g / 1 ¾ oz / ⅓ cup peas, thawed if frozen

100 ml / 3 ½ fl. oz / ½ cup vegetable stock

2 tbsp rice wine

2 tbsp soy sauce

handful of coriander (cilantro), chopped

METHOD

1. Cook the noodles as per the packet instructions, drain and set aside.

2. Heat half the oil in a wok over a medium heat. Mix the eggs with the sesame oil and cook in the hot wok for 1-2 minutes to make an omelette. Remove and slice.

3. Add the remaining oil to the pan and fry the ginger, garlic and chilli for 1 minute until fragrant.

4. Add the mushrooms and peas to the pan and continue to stir-fry for 2-3 minutes until softened and starting to colour.

5. Combine the stock, wine and soy. Pour into the pan and toss the ingredients to coat. Add the noodles to the pan and continue to cook and stir for 2-3 minutes. Return the egg to the pan to heat through and toss the coriander through, reserving some as a garnish.

6. Divide between serving bowls and top with the reserved coriander.

Spicy noodles with spring onions

SERVES: 4 | PREP TIME: 5 MINUTES | COOKING TIME: 10 MINUTES

INGREDIENTS

400 g / 14 oz medium egg noodles

3 spring onions (scallions), sliced

1 clove of garlic, crushed

50 ml / 1 ¾ fl. oz / ¼ cup chinkiang (black rice) vinegar

50 ml / 1 ¾ fl. oz / ¼ cup chilli oil

50 ml / 1 ¾ fl. oz / ¼ cup sweet chilli sauce

2 tbsp light soy sauce

METHOD

1. Cook the noodles according to the packet instructions, then drain well.

2. Meanwhile, put the spring onions and garlic in a warm serving bowl and whisk in the vinegar, chilli oil, chilli sauce and soy sauce.

3. Toss with the hot noodles and serve immediately.

Kimchi soup

SERVES: 2-4 | PREP TIME: 10 MINUTES | COOKING TIME: 20 MINUTES

INGREDIENTS

1 tsp vegetable oil

1 carrot, diced

1 shallot, diced

1 clove of garlic, minced

½ tsp turmeric

50 g / 1 ¾ oz spring greens, chopped

1 l / 35 fl. oz / 4 cups chicken stock

300 g / 10 ½ oz kimchi (see recipe in
Vegetable Dishes)

1 tbsp sesame seeds

1 tbsp black sesame seeds

METHOD

1. In a large saucepan heat the oil over a
   medium heat and sweat the carrot, shallot
   and garlic together for 4-5 minutes
   until softened.

2. Stir through the turmeric and greens before
   adding the chicken stock. Turn up the heat
   until boiling before turning back down to a
   simmer for 8-10 minutes. Season.

3. Add the kimchi to the soup and continue to
   cook for a further 4-5 minutes until warmed
   through. Spoon into serving bowls and
   sprinkle over the sesame seeds.

189

Wheat gluten noodle soup

SERVES: 4 | PREP TIME: 5 MINUTES | COOKING TIME: 10 MINUTES

INGREDIENTS

300 g / 10 ½ oz wheat noodles

1 litre / 1 pint 14 fl. oz / 4 cups vegetable stock

2 tbsp Shaoxing rice wine

2 tbsp light soy sauce

1 tsp caster (superfine) sugar

150 g / 3 ½ oz / 2 cups wheat gluten (rehydrated if dried), cubed

175 g / 6 oz / 2 cups shiitake mushrooms, sliced

3 spring onions (scallions), chopped, green parts only

2 large red chillies (chilies), sliced

2 tsp sesame seeds

METHOD

1. Cook the noodles in boiling water according to the packet instructions or until al dente. Plunge into cold water, then drain well and divide between four bowls.

2. Heat the stock in a saucepan with the rice wine, soy sauce and sugar. When it starts to boil, add the wheat gluten and shiitakes and simmer for 2 minutes.

3. Ladle the soup over the noodles and serve, garnished with spring onion greens, chillies and sesame seeds.

Garlic and ginger fried rice

SERVES: 4 | PREP TIME: 5 MINUTES | COOKING TIME: 25 MINUTES

INGREDIENTS

450 g / 1 lb / 2 ¼ cups long-grain rice

2 tbsp vegetable oil

3 cloves of garlic, finely chopped

1 ½ tbsp root ginger, finely chopped

1 tbsp light soy sauce

1 tsp sesame oil

METHOD

1. Put the rice in a saucepan and add enough water to cover it by 1 cm. Bring the pan to the boil then cover and turn down the heat to its lowest setting.

2. Cook for 10 minutes then turn off the heat and leave to stand, without lifting the lid, for 10 minutes.

3. Heat the vegetable oil in a large wok and fry the garlic and ginger for 1 minute.

4. Add the rice and stir-fry for 2 minutes. Season the rice with soy sauce and sesame oil, then serve immediately.

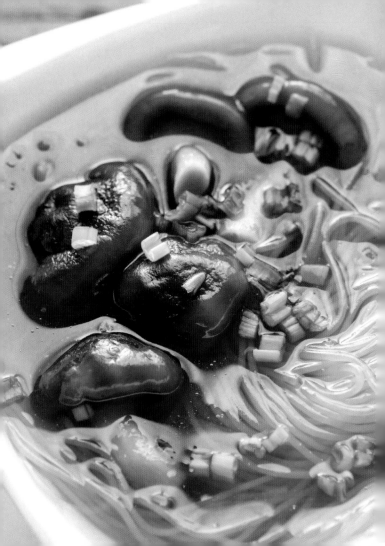

Shiitake and glass noodle soup

SERVES: 4 | PREP TIME: 1 HOUR | COOKING TIME: 10 MINUTES

INGREDIENTS

20 small dried shiitake mushrooms

300 g / 10 ½ oz glass noodles

1 tbsp vegetable oil

1 tbsp fresh root ginger, finely chopped

2 tbsp light soy sauce

2 tbsp chinkiang (black rice) vinegar

½ tsp ground white pepper

1 tsp cornflour (cornstarch)

1 tsp sesame oil

3 spring onions (scallions), finely chopped,
green parts only

METHOD

1. Cover the shiitake mushrooms in 1.2 litres of boiling water and leave to soak for 1 hour.

2. Meanwhile, cook the noodles in boiling water according to the packet instructions or until al dente. Plunge into cold water, then drain well and divide between four bowls.

3. Remove the mushrooms from the soaking water and dry thoroughly with kitchen paper. Strain the soaking liquor through a muslin-lined sieve and set aside.

4. Heat the vegetable oil in a large wok and fry the ginger for 30 seconds. Add the shiitakes and stir-fry for 2 minutes.

5. Pour in the strained soaking liquor and add the soy sauce, vinegar and white pepper. Slake the cornflour with 1 tablespoon of cold water, then stir it into the soup.

6. When the soup simmers and thickens, add the sesame oil and spring onion greens, then taste and adjust the seasoning with salt and white pepper. Ladle over the noodles and serve immediately.

Vegetable and noodle broth

SERVES: 2-4 | PREP TIME: 15 MINUTES | COOKING TIME: 20 MINUTES

INGREDIENTS

200 g / 7 oz egg noodles

25 ml / ¾ fl. oz soy sauce

2 tbsp mirin

1 tsp dark sesame oil

2 cloves of garlic, minced

15 g / ½ oz ginger, grated

1 tbsp sugar

25 ml / ¾ fl. oz rice vinegar

1 tsp chilli (chili) flakes

800 ml / 27 fl. oz / 3 ⅓ cups chicken stock

200 g / 7 oz bean sprouts

bunch of spring onions (scallions), sliced

2 carrots, grated

1 head of cauliflower, florets chopped

25 g / 1 oz / ¼ cup cashew nuts, chopped

METHOD

1. Cook the noodles as per the packet instructions, then drain and set aside.

2. Place the soy, mirin, sesame oil, garlic, ginger, sugar, vinegar and chilli into a saucepan with the stock.

3. Heat over a moderately high heat until boiling, then reduce to a high simmer and cook for 12-15 minutes.

4. Add the bean sprouts, spring onions, carrots and cauliflower and continue to cook for a further 10-12 minutes until the vegetables are tender.

5. Place the noodles into serving bowls and top with the soup and vegetables. Sprinkle over the chopped nuts as garnish.

Egg-fried rice

SERVES: 4 | PREP TIME: 5 MINUTES | COOKING TIME: 8 MINUTES

INGREDIENTS

2 tbsp vegetable oil

1 clove of garlic, crushed

1 tbsp root ginger, finely chopped

2 spring onions (scallions), chopped

1 large egg

75 g / 2 ½ oz / ½ cup frozen peas, defrosted

1 handful bean sprouts

500 g / 17 ½ oz / 3 cups long-grain rice, cooked and cooled

1 tbsp light soy sauce

1 tsp sesame oil

METHOD

1.   Heat the vegetable oil in a large wok
and fry the garlic, ginger and spring onions
for 30 seconds.

2.   Add the egg and stir to scramble. Add the
peas and bean sprouts and stir-fry
for 1 minute.

3.   Add the rice and stir-fry until piping hot –
this should take about 4 minutes.

4.   Season the rice with soy sauce, sesame oil
and black pepper, then serve immediately.

Sesame balls with red bean paste

MAKES: 12 | PREP TIME: 30 MINUTES | COOKING TIME: 3 MINUTES

INGREDIENTS

125 g / 4 ½ oz / ¾ cup muscovado sugar

450 g / 1 lb / 3 cups glutinous rice flour

200 g / 7 oz / 1 cup sweet red bean paste

75 g / 2 ½ oz / ½ cup white sesame seeds

vegetable oil, for deep-frying

METHOD

1. Dissolve the sugar in 250 ml of boiling water. Sieve the flour into a mixing bowl, then gradually incorporate the sugar water, adding a little extra boiling water if needed.

2. Divide the dough into 12 pieces and roll each one into a ball. Flatten the balls and add a spoonful of red bean paste to the centre of each one. Gather up the edges to completely enclose the filling. Dip the balls in a little cold water, then roll in sesame seeds to coat.

3. Heat the oil in a deep fat fryer, according to the manufacturer's instructions, to a temperature of 180°C (350F). Deep fry in batches of three for 3 minutes, or until they turn golden brown and rise to the surface.

Rice noodles with pickled vegetable

SERVES: 2 | PREP TIME: 30 MINUTES | COOKING TIME: 15 MINUTES

INGREDIENTS

½ onion, sliced

2 red peppers, sliced

2 carrots, shredded

2 tbsp rice vinegar

2 tbsp rice wine

1 tsp sugar

1 tsp salt

300 g / 10 ½ oz rice noodles

1 tbsp sesame oil

1 tbsp light soy sauce

small bunch of coriander (cilantro), chopped

METHOD

1. Place the onion, peppers and carrots into a bowl.

2. Whisk together the vinegar, rice wine, sugar and salt. Pour over the vegetables and add enough water to just cover. Cover the bowl and set aside for 30 minutes.

3. Cook the noodles in boiling water as per the packet instructions. Drain well before tossing through the sesame oil, soy and most of the coriander.

4. Remove the vegetables from the liquid and shake off any excess. Serve the noodles with the pickled vegetables and garnish with the remaining coriander.

Oyster sauce soup

SERVES: 2-4 | PREP TIME: 10 MINUTES | COOKING TIME: 15 MINUTES

INGREDIENTS

2 tbsp oyster sauce

1 tbsp soy sauce

800 ml / 27 fl. oz / 3 ⅓ cups chicken stock

10 g / ⅓ oz ginger, sliced

2 cloves of garlic, sliced

100 g / 3 ½ oz napa cabbage, sliced

1 lime, juice and zest

200 g / 7 oz egg noodles

2 tbsp sesame seeds

1 tbsp sesame oil

METHOD

1. Place the oyster sauce, soy sauce, stock, ginger and garlic into a saucepan. Heat until boiling and then reduce to a high simmer.

2. Add the cabbage and lime to the soup and simmer for 8-10 minutes

3. Cook the noodles as per the packet instructions, drain and set aside.

4. Add the noodles to the soup with the sesame seeds and oil.

5. Spoon into serving bowls and serve with crispy wontons or dumplings to dip into the soup.

199

Vegetable rice bowl

SERVES: 1 | PREP TIME: 15 MINUTES | COOKING TIME: 25 MINUTES

INGREDIENTS

80 g / 2 ¾ oz / ⅓ cup long-grain rice

2 carrots

½ cucumber

½ avocado

25 g / 1 oz crispy seaweed

1 tsp sesame seeds

1 tsp black sesame seeds

25 g / 1 oz pickled ginger

2 tbsp soy sauce

METHOD

1. Cook the rice as per the packet instructions, drain and set aside.

2. Slice the carrots and cucumber into ribbons using a mandoline or sharp knife. Roll the ribbons into tubes.

3. Slice the avocado, removing the stone.

4. Arrange the rice, carrot, cucumber and avocado in a serving bowl and top with the seaweed and sesame seeds.

5. Serve with the ginger and soy on the side for dipping.

Hot pepper relish

SERVES: 2-4 | PREP TIME: 10 MINUTES | COOKING TIME: 10 MINUTES

INGREDIENTS

4 red chillies (chili)

2 shallots

1 red pepper

2 cloves of garlic

25 ml / ¾ fl. oz rice wine vinegar

25 g / 1 oz caster (superfine) sugar

METHOD

1. Roughly chop the chillies, shallots and pepper. Place into the cup of a blender and pulse once or twice.

2. Add the garlic, vinegar and sugar before pulsing a couple more times to combine.

3. Pour the relish into a saucepan and place over a moderate heat for 10 minutes to reduce the liquid and intensify the flavour.

4. Remove from the heat and stir through the salt to taste.

Red curry laksa

SERVES: 2-4 | PREP TIME: 15 MINUTES | COOKING TIME: 15 MINUTES

INGREDIENTS

4 red chillies (chili)

2 cloves of garlic

15 g / ½ oz ginger, peeled and roughly chopped

1 lime, juice and zest

2 tbsp cashew nuts

1 tsp chilli (chili) flakes

2 tbsp vegetable oil

2 shallots, roughly chopped

400 ml / 13 ½ fl. oz / 1 ⅔ cups coconut milk

400 ml / 13 ½ fl. oz / 1 ⅔ cups vegetable stock

2 tsp sugar

1 tsp fish sauce

1 tsp soy sauce

2 tbsp sesame seeds

2 tbsp black sesame seeds

1 tbsp sesame oil

METHOD

1. Place the chillies, garlic, ginger, lime, nuts, chilli flakes, vegetable oil and shallots into a blender. Blend to form a paste, adding a little more oil or lime to thin if necessary.

2. Place saucepan over a medium high heat. Add the paste and fry for 2-3 minutes until fragrant.

3. Add the coconut milk, stock, sugar, fish sauce and soy to the pan. Heat until boiling, then reduce to a simmer for 8-10 minutes.

4. Taste to check the seasoning, adding more sugar or soy to adjust the taste.

5. Spoon into serving bowls and sprinkle over the sesame seeds and a drizzle of sesame oil.

Vegetable dumplings

SERVES: 4 | PREP TIME: 45 MINUTES | COOKING TIME: 14 MINUTES

INGREDIENTS

175 g / 6 oz / 1 ¼ cups plain (all-purpose) flour

225 g / 8 oz / 1 ½ cups firm tofu, finely diced

1 carrot, coarsely grated

½ red pepper, finely chopped

2 savoy cabbage leaves, deveined and
finely chopped

2 spring onions (scallions), finely chopped

1 tsp fresh root ginger, finely grated

100 g / 3 ½ oz / ½ cup canned water chestnuts,
finely chopped

1 tbsp light soy sauce

1 tsp caster (superfine) sugar

1 tsp sesame oil

1 tsp cornflour (cornstarch)

1 egg white, beaten

METHOD

1. Sift the flour into a bowl and stir in 160 ml of
   recently boiled water. Knead for 8 minutes or
   until smooth, adding more flour if necessary.
   Rest for 30 minutes.

2. Meanwhile, mix the tofu with the carrot,
   pepper, cabbage, spring onions, ginger,
   water chestnuts, soy sauce, sugar, sesame oil
   and cornflour. Season with 1 teaspoon
   of salt and some freshly ground
   white pepper.

3. Divide the rested dough into 24 balls, then
   roll out each one into an 8 cm (3 in) circle on
   a floured surface.

4. Put a heaped teaspoon of filling in the centre
   of each circle, then brush round the edge
   with egg white. Gather up the edges and
   twist round to seal.

5. Space out the dumplings in oiled steamer
   baskets and steam for 10 minutes,
   then serve immediately.

Hot and sour noodle soup

SERVES: 4 | PREP TIME: 20 MINUTES | COOKING TIME: 5 MINUTE

INGREDIENTS

300 g / 10 ½ oz wide rice noodles

4 red chillies (chilies), sliced

2 cloves of garlic, chopped

1 tbsp fresh root ginger, chopped

1 tbsp vegetable oil

1 litre / 1 pint 14 fl. oz / 4 cups vegetable stock

2 tbsp Shaoxing rice wine

2 tsp caster (superfine) sugar

1 lime, juiced

1 tbsp light soy sauce, plus extra to serve

4 lettuce leaves

200 g / 7 oz / 1 ⅓ cups tofu, julienned

½ red onion, sliced

few sprigs of mint

METHOD

1. Cook the noodles in boiling water accord
   to the packet instructions or until al den
   Plunge into cold water, then drain well a
   divide between four bowls.

2. Pound three of the chillies in a pestle an
   mortar with a pinch of salt to a fine past
   Add the garlic and pound again, followed
   the ginger.

3. Heat the oil in a large wok and stir-fry th
   paste for 2 minutes. Add the stock, rice wi
   sugar, lime juice and soy sauce and
   bring to the boil.

4. Ladle the stock over the noodles and garn
   each bowl with a lettuce leaf, a pile of tof
   some sliced red onion, the remaining chi
   and a few sprigs of mint. Serve with extra s
   sauce at the table for people to adjust the
   own seasoning.

Vegetarian summer rolls

SERVES: 4 | PREP TIME: 20 MINUTES

INGREDIENTS

6 rice paper wrappers

6 soft lettuce leaves

¼ cucumber, cut into batons

1 carrot, coarsely grated

3 red cabbage leaves, shredded

1 tbsp black and white sesame seeds

edible flowers, to garnish

METHOD

1. Dip the first rice paper wrapper in a bow
   cold water, then lay it out on a clean
   chopping board. Lay a lettuce leaf on top
   add some cucumber, carrot and cabbag

2. Fold over the sides of the wrapper, then r
   up to enclose the filling.

3. Repeat with the rest of the ingredients
   form six rolls, then cut them into bite-si
   pieces. Sprinkle with sesame seeds and s
   immediately, garnished with edible flow

4. Delicious served as a starter or snack.

Sesame seaweed salad

SERVES: 4 | PREP TIME: 10 MINUTES | COOKING TIME: 2 MINUTES

INGREDIENTS

50 g / 1 ¾ oz / 1 cup dried wakame seaweed

1 tbsp sesame seeds

1 tsp Chinese sesame paste

1 tsp runny honey

1 tsp light soy sauce

1 tsp rice wine vinegar

METHOD

1. Put the dried seaweed in a bowl and cover in hot water. Leave to soak for 5 minutes, then drain well and refresh in cold water. Drain.

2. Dry-fry the sesame seeds in a large wok until lightly toasted, then scrape them into a bowl and set aside.

3. Mix the sesame paste with the honey, soy sauce and vinegar.

4. Toss the seaweed in the dressing and serve sprinkled with sesame seeds.

Soy glazed lotus roots

SERVES: 2 | PREP TIME: 10 MINUTES | COOKING TIME: 1 HOUR

INGREDIENTS

300 g / 10 ½ oz lotus root, peeled and sliced

50 ml / 1 ¾ fl. oz / ¼ cup soy sauce

1 tbsp soft brown sugar

2 tsp sesame oil

2 spring onions (scallions), sliced

2 tsp sesame seeds

METHOD

1. Place the lotus root into a pan and cover with water. Heat until boiling and then reduce to a simmer for 20 minutes.

2. Strain the lotus root and rinse with cold water.

3. Place the lotus root into a clean pan and add the soy sauce, brown sugar and sesame oil. Add enough water to cover the lotus root and place onto a moderately high heat until boiling. Reduce to a simmer and cook for around 40 minutes, stirring occasionally.

4. Turn the heat up to moderately high and reduce the liquid down to a glaze, turning the lotus root in the liquid to coat.

5. 5. Place onto a serving dish and garnish with the spring onions and sesame seeds.

Mushroom fried rice

SERVES: 4 | PREP TIME: 2 MINUTES | COOKING TIME: 10-15 MINUTES

INGREDIENTS

1 ½ cups long-grain rice

3 tbsp cooking oil

1 ½ lb shiitake mushrooms, stems removed, caps sliced

¼ tsp dried red pepper flakes

1 tbsp grated fresh ginger

6 spring onions including green tops, chopped

¼ cup soy sauce

1 tsp sesame oil

METHOD

1. Bring a medium pot of salted water to a boil. Stir in the rice and cook according to manufacturer's instructions. Drain and set aside to cool.

2. Meanwhile, in a large pan, heat 1 tablespoon of the oil over moderate heat. Add half the mushrooms and cook for 5 minutes, stirring frequently, until the mushrooms are tender and golden. Transfer to a plate. Repeat with the remaining mushrooms and another tablespoon of the oil. Add the mushrooms to the plate.

3. Heat the remaining cooking oil over a moderate heat. Add the red pepper flakes, ginger, and scallions and cook for about 30 seconds. Increase the heat to moderately high and add the rice and soy sauce. Add salt to season. Cook, stirring, for 2 minutes and then add the mushrooms. Cook, stirring, until everything's warm, for another 2 minutes. Stir in the sesame oil.

Oyster mushroom salad

SERVES: 1 | PREP TIME: 10 MINUTES | COOKING TIME: 10 MINUTES

INGREDIENTS

100 g / 3 ½ oz oyster mushrooms

1 tsp vegetable oil

1 clove of garlic, sliced

1 tsp chilli (chili) flakes

1 red pepper, sliced

1 tsp soy sauce

1 tsp sesame seeds

50 g / 1 ¾ oz crisp seaweed

METHOD

1. Slice the mushrooms, keeping them fairly large.

2. Heat the oil in a wok over a medium heat. Add the garlic and fry for 30 seconds before adding the mushrooms, chilli and pepper.

3. Quickly stir-fry, adding the soy sauce as seasoning. Toss through the sesame seeds.

4. Place into a serving bowl and top with the crispy seaweed.

Steamed sesame balls

ERVES: 12 | PREP TIME: 2 HOURS 35 MINUTES | COOKING TIME: 12 MINUTES

INGREDIENTS

300 g / 10 ½ oz / 2 cups plain (all-purpose) flour

150 g / 5 ½ oz / 1 cup cornflour (cornstarch)

75 g / 2 ½ oz / ⅓ cup dark muscovado sugar

1 tsp easy blend dried yeast

50 ml / 1 ¾ fl. oz / ¼ cup sesame oil

2 ½ tsp baking powder

75 g / 2 ½ oz / ½ cup white sesame seeds

METHOD

1. Mix the flour with the cornflour, sugar and yeast. Stir the oil into 200 ml of warm water, then stir it into the flour.

2. Knead the dough for 10 minutes, then cover and leave to rise for 2 hours. Knead the baking powder into the dough and leave to rest for 15 minutes.

3. Divide the dough into twelve equal balls. Roll each one in sesame seeds to coat, then transfer to a square of greaseproof paper.

4. Steam the buns on the paper squares for 12 minutes, ensuring there is plenty of room for them to expand. Serve warm.

Crispy seaweed

SERVES: 6 | PREP TIME: 10 MINUTES | COOKING TIME: 2 MINUTES

INGREDIENTS

150 g / 5 ½ oz / 4 ½ cups spring (collard) greens
or kale

vegetable oil, for deep frying

1 tsp caster (superfine) sugar

1 pinch Chinese five spice

METHOD

1. Remove the tough central veins of the greens, then shred or chop the rest.

2. Blanch the greens in boiling salted water for 1 minute, then drain well. Tip onto a clean tea towel and dry thoroughly. Any leftover moisture will make the oil spit.

3. Heat the oil in a deep fat fryer according to the manufacturer's instructions to a temperature of 180°C (350F).

4. Deep fry the greens in batches for 30 seconds or until crisp, then drain on plenty of kitchen paper.

5. Mix the sugar and five spice with ½ teaspoon of salt and sprinkle it on top of the 'seaweed'.

Sticky tofu poke bowl

SERVES: 1 | PREP TIME: 20 MINUTES | COOKING TIME: 20 MINUTES

INGREDIENTS

150 g / 5 ¼ oz tofu

1 tsp honey

1 tsp soy sauce

½ lime, juiced

1 tsp oyster sauce

1 tsp Sichuan pepper, crushed

100 g / 3 ½ oz glass noodles

75 g / 2 ½ oz edamame beans

1 carrot, cut into ribbons

¼ cucumber, sliced

¼ watermelon radish, sliced

METHOD

1. Preheat the oven to 180°C (160°C fan) / 350F / gas 4. Line a baking tray with foil.

2. Wash and pat dry the tofu before slicing. Combine the honey, soy, lime, oyster sauce and pepper. Coat the tofu in the marinade and set aside for 10 minutes.

3. Place the tofu onto the baking tray and cook for 12-15 minutes until sticky and charred at the edges. Turn once during cooking and baste with any leftover marinade.

4. Cook the noodles as per instructions, them drain and set aside. Boil the edamame beans in water for 4-5 minutes. Drain and shell.

5. Place the glass noodles into a bowl and top with the tofu, beans, carrot, cucumber and radish.

Shiitake and ginger soup

SERVES: 2-4 | PREP TIME: 10 MINUTES | COOKING TIME: 10 MINUTES

INGREDIENTS

200 g / 7 oz shiitake mushrooms, roughly chopped

25 g / 1 oz ginger, chopped

2 cloves of garlic, sliced

2 tbsp dark soy sauce

1 tbsp oyster sauce

800 ml / 27 fl. oz / 3 1/3 cups / 27 fl. oz chicken stock

4 spring onions (scallions), sliced

200 g / 7 oz egg noodles

METHOD

1. Place the ingredients, excluding the noodles, into a saucepan. Heat over a high heat until boiling before reducing to a simmer.

2. Cook for 18-20 minutes until the mushrooms are tender and the flavours have intensified.

3. Cook the noodles as per the packet instructions, drain and set aside.

4. Divide the noodles into serving bowls before spooning over the soup.

Kimchi fried rice

SERVES: 4 | PREP TIME: 5 MINUTES | COOKING TIME: 10 MINUTES

INGREDIENTS

2 tbsp vegetable oil

1 small onion, finely chopped

2 cloves of garlic, crushed

1 tbsp root ginger, finely chopped

1 red pepper, deseeded, quartered and sliced

200 g / 7 oz / 1 ¾ cups kimchi (see recipe in Vegetable Dishes)

500 g / 17 ½ oz / 3 cups jasmine rice, cooked and cooled

2 tbsp light soy sauce

2 tsp sesame oil

small bunch Chinese chives, cut into short lengths

METHOD

1. Heat the vegetable oil in a large wok and fry the onion, garlic and ginger for 2 minutes.

2. Add the red pepper and fry for 2 minutes.

3. Chop the kimchi and add to the rice and stir-fry until piping hot – this should take about 4 minutes.

4. Season the rice with soy sauce, sesame oil and black pepper, then serve immediately, garnished with Chinese chives.

Aubergine with ginger and spring onion

SERVES: 4 | PREP TIME: 20 MINUTES | COOKING TIME: 25 MINUTES

INGREDIENTS

2 aubergines (eggplants),
cut into thick batons

2 tbsp vegetable oil

2 tbsp cornflour (cornstarch)

1 tbsp fresh root ginger, cut into a
fine julienne

4 spring onions (scallions), sliced,
green and white parts separated

2 tbsp light soy sauce

1 tsp caster (superfine) sugar

50 ml / 1 ¾ fl. oz / ¼ cup Shaoxing
rice wine

METHOD

1. Dissolve 1 tablespoon of salt in 1 litre of
    water. Add the aubergines and stir well, then
    sit a plate on top to keep them submerged.
    Leave to soak for 15 minutes, then drain well
    and squeeze dry with plenty of
    kitchen paper.

2. Heat 1 tablespoon of the oil in a large
    wok over a medium heat. Coat the aubergine
    with 1 ½ tablespoons of the cornflour, then
    add a single layer of batons to the wok and
    fry in batches until browned all over.
    Transfer finished batches to a plate
    and reserve.

3. Add the rest of the oil to the wok and fry the
    ginger and spring onion whites for
    2 minutes. Stir the rest of the cornflour into
    the soy sauce, sugar and rice wine, then add
    it to the wok and stir for 2 minutes.

4. Add the aubergine batons and stir carefully
    over a medium heat until well coated. Spoon
    into serving bowls and serve garnished with
    the spring onion greens.

Spicy vegetable stir-fry

SERVES: 4 | PREP TIME: 5 MINUTES | COOKING TIME: 8 MINUTES

INGREDIENTS

2 tbsp sesame seeds

2 tbsp vegetable oil

1 red onion, quartered and thinly sliced

3 red chillies (chilies), sliced

2 cloves of garlic, crushed

1 tbsp root ginger, finely chopped

½ tsp ground Szechwan pepper

1 red pepper, deseeded and thinly sliced

1 orange pepper, deseeded and
thinly sliced

1 Chinese aubergine (eggplant),
halved and thinly sliced

1 head broccoli, cut into small florets

100 g / 3 ½ oz / 1 cup oyster mushrooms,
cut into strips

2 tbsp light soy sauce

2 tsp sesame oil

1 handful fresh coriander (cilantro) leaves

METHOD

1. Dry-fry the sesame seeds in a large wok until
   lightly toasted, then scrape them into a bowl
   and set aside.

2. Heat the vegetable oil in the wok and fry the
   onion, chillies, garlic and ginger for 2 minutes.

3. Sprinkle in the Szechwan pepper, then add
   the vegetables and fry for 4 minutes.

4. Add the mushrooms and stir-fry for
   1 minute, then season with soy sauce and
   sesame oil.

5. Serve the stir-fry with rice or noodles and
   sprinkle with the toasted sesame seeds and
   some coriander leaves.

INDEX